Contents

Contents

SECTION I:
GW-BASIC
User's Guide

Chapter 1
Welcome to GW-BASIC

Microsoft® GW-BASIC® is a simple, easy-to-learn, easy-to-use computer programming language with English-like statements and mathematical notations. With GW-BASIC you will be able to write both simple and complex programs to run on your computer. You will also be able to modify existing software that is written in GW-BASIC.

This book is designed to help you use the GW-BASIC Interpreter with the MS-DOS® operating system. Section 1.5 lists resources that will teach you how to program.

1.1   System Requirements

This version of GW-BASIC requires MS-DOS version 3.2 or later.

1.2   Preliminaries

Your GW-BASIC files will be on the MS-DOS diskette located at the back of the *MS-DOS User's Reference*. Be sure to make a working copy of the diskette before you proceed.

Note

This book is written for the user familiar with the MS-DOS operating system. For more information on MS-DOS, refer to the *Microsoft MS-DOS User's Guide* and *User's Reference* or *Running MS-DOS* by Van Wolverton (Microsoft Press, 1989).

1.3 Notational Conventions

Throughout this manual, the following conventions are used to distinguish elements of text:

bold   Used for commands, options, switches, and literal portions of syntax that must appear exactly as shown.

italic   Used for filenames, variables, and placeholders that represent the type of text to be entered by the user.

monospace   Used for sample command lines, program code and examples, and sample sessions.

SMALL CAPS   Used for keys, key sequences, and acronyms.

Brackets surround optional command-line elements.

1.4 Organization of This Book

The GW-BASIC *User's Guide and Reference* is divided into two sections. Section I: "GW-BASIC User's Guide" includes the following six chapters:

Chapter 1, "Welcome to GW-BASIC," describes this book.

Chapter 2, "Getting Started With GW-BASIC," is an elementary guideline on how to begin programming.

Chapter 3, "Reviewing and Practicing GW-BASIC," lets you use the principles of GW-BASIC explained in Chapter 2.

Chapter 4, "The GW-BASIC Screen Editor," discusses editing commands that can be used when inputting or modifying a GW-BASIC program. It also explains the unique properties of the ten redefinable function keys and of other keys and keystroke combinations.

Chapter 5, "Creating and Using Files," tells you how to create files and to use the diskette input/output (I/O) procedures.

Chapter 6, "Constants, Variables, Expressions, and Operators," defines the elements of GW-BASIC and describes how you will use them.

Section II: "GW-BASIC User's Reference" is an alphabetical reference to GW-BASIC instructions that includes statements, functions, commands, and variables. The name and type of each instruction is listed at the top of the page, and is followed by:

Purpose	The purpose of the instruction
Syntax	The complete notation of the instruction
Comments	Pertinent information about the instruction, and what happens when it is encountered by GW-BASIC
Examples	An illustration of the instruction as it might appear in a program

Any special information about an instruction is also included in the "Notes" portion of the description.

This book also includes the following appendixes and a glossary:

Appendix A, "Error Codes and Messages," is a summary of all the error codes and error messages that you might encounter while using GW-BASIC.

Appendix B, "Mathematical Functions," describes how to calculate certain mathematical functions not intrinsic to GW-BASIC.

Appendix C, "ASCII Character Codes," lists the ASCII character codes recognized by GW-BASIC.

Appendix D, "Assembly Language (Machine Code) Subroutines," shows how to include assembly language subroutines with GW-BASIC.

Appendix E, "Converting BASIC Programs to GW-BASIC," provides pointers on converting programs written in BASIC to GW-BASIC.

Appendix F, "Communications," describes the GW-BASIC statements required to support RS-232 asynchronous communications with other computers and peripheral devices.

Appendix G, "Hexadecimal Equivalents," lists decimal and binary equivalents to hexadecimal values.

Appendix H, "Key Scan Codes," lists and illustrates the key scan code values used in GW-BASIC.

Appendix I, "Characters Recognized by GW-BASIC," describes the GW-BASIC character set.

The Glossary defines words and phrases commonly used in GW-BASIC and data processing.

1.5 Bibliography

This book is a guide to the use of the GW-BASIC Interpreter; it makes no attempt to teach the BASIC programming language. The following texts may be useful for those who wish to learn BASIC programming:

Albrecht, Robert L., and Don Inman. *GW-BASIC Made Easy*. Berkeley, Calif.: Osborne/McGraw-Hill, 1989.

Coan, James. *Basic BASIC*. 2d ed. Rochelle Park, N.J.: Hayden Book Company, 1978.

Dwyer, Thomas A., and Margot Critchfield. *BASIC and the Personal Computer*. Reading, Mass.: Addison-Wesley Publishing Co., 1978.

Ettlin, Walter A., and Gregory Solberg. *The MBASIC Handbook*. Berkeley, Calif.: Osborne/McGraw-Hill, 1983.

Chapter 2
Getting Started
With GW-BASIC

This chapter describes how to load GW-BASIC into your system. It also explains the two different types of operation modes, line formats, and the various elements of GW-BASIC.

2.1   Loading GW-BASIC

To use the GW-BASIC language, you must load it into the memory of your computer from your working copy of the MS-DOS diskette. Use the following procedure:

1. Turn on your computer.

2. Insert your working copy of the MS-DOS diskette into Drive A of your computer, and press RETURN.

3. Type the following command after the A> prompt, and press RETURN:

```
gwbasic
```

Once you enter GW-BASIC, the GW-BASIC prompt, *Ok*, will replace the MS-DOS prompt, *A>*.

On the screen, the line *XXXXX Bytes Free* indicates how many bytes are available for use in memory while using GW-BASIC.

The function key (F1–F10) assignments appear on the bottom line of the screen. These function keys can be used to eliminate key strokes and save you time. Chapter 4, "The GW-BASIC Screen Editor," contains detailed information on function keys.

2.2   Modes of Operation

Once GW-BASIC is initialized (loaded), it displays the *Ok* prompt. *Ok* means GW-BASIC is at *command level*; that is, it is ready to accept commands. At this point, GW-BASIC may be used in either of two modes: *direct mode* or *indirect mode*.

2.2.1   Direct Mode

In the direct mode, GW-BASIC statements and commands are executed as they are entered. Results of arithmetic and logical operations can be displayed immediately and/or stored for later use, but the instructions themselves are lost after execution. This mode is useful for debugging and for using GW-BASIC as a calculator for quick computations that do not require a complete program.

2.2.2   Indirect Mode

The indirect mode is used to enter programs. Program lines are always preceded by line numbers, and are stored in memory. The program stored in memory is executed by entering the RUN command.

2.3   The GW-BASIC Command Line Format

The GW-BASIC command line lets you change the environment or the conditions that apply while using GW-BASIC.

Note

> When you specify modifications to the operating environment of GW-BASIC, be sure to maintain the parameter sequence shown in the syntax statement. To skip a parameter, insert a comma. This will let the computer know that you have no changes to that particular parameter.

GW-BASIC uses a command line of the following form:

gwbasic[*filename*][<*stdin*][[>]>*stdout*][/**f**:*n*][/**i**][/**s**:*n*][/**c**:*n*][/**m**:[*n*][,*n*]][/**d**]

filename is the name of a GW-BASIC program file. If this parameter is present, GW-BASIC proceeds as if a RUN command had been given. If no extension is provided for the filename, a default file extension of .BAS is assumed. The .BAS extension indicates that the file is a GW-BASIC file. The maximum number of characters a filename may contain is eight with a decimal and three extension characters.

<stdin redirects GW-BASIC's standard input to be read from the specified file. When used, it must appear before any switches.

This might be used when you have multiple files that might be used by your program and you wish to specify a particular input file.

>stdout redirects GW-BASIC's standard output to the specified file or device. When used, it must appear before any switches. Using $>>$ before *stdout* causes output to be appended.

GW-BASIC can be redirected to read from standard input (keyboard) and write to standard output (screen) by providing the input and output filenames on the command line as follows:

gwbasic *program name <input file[>]>output file*

An explanation of file redirection follows this discussion of the GW-BASIC command line.

Switches appear frequently in command lines; they designate a specified course of action for the command, as opposed to using the default for that setting. A switch parameter is preceded by a slash (/).

/f:*n* sets the maximum number of files that may be opened simultaneously during the execution of a GW-BASIC program. Each file requires 194 bytes for the File Control Block (FCB) plus 128 bytes for the data buffer. The data buffer size may be altered with the **/s:** switch. If the **/f:** switch is omitted, the maximum number of open files defaults to 3. This switch is ignored unless the **/i** switch is also specified on the command line.

/i makes GW-BASIC statically allocate space required for file operations, based on the **/s** and **/f** switches.

/s:*n* sets the maximum record length allowed for use with files. The record length option in the OPEN statement cannot exceed this value. If the **/s:** switch is omitted, the record length defaults to 128 bytes. The maximum record size is 32767.

/c:*n* controls RS-232 communications. If RS-232 cards are present, /c:0 disables RS-232 support, and any subsequent I/O attempts for each RS-232 card present. If the **/c:** switch is omitted, 256 bytes are allocated for the receive buffer and 128 bytes for the transmit buffer for each card present.

The /c: switch has no affect when RS-232 cards are not present. The /c:n switch allocates n bytes for the receive buffer and 128 bytes for the transmit buffer for each RS-232 card present.

/**m**:n[,n] sets the highest memory location (first n) and maximum block size (second n) used by GW-BASIC. GW-BASIC attempts to allocate 64K bytes of memory for the data and stack segments. If machine language subroutines are to be used with GW-BASIC programs, use the /**m**: switch to set the highest location that GW-BASIC can use. The maximum block size is in multiples of 16. It is used to reserve space for user programs (assembly language subroutines) beyond GW-BASIC's workspace.

The default for maximum block size is the highest memory location. The default for the highest memory location is 64K bytes unless maximum block size is specified, in which case the default is the maximum block size (in multiples of 16).

/**d** allows certain functions to return double-precision results. When the /**d** switch is specified, approximately 3000 bytes of additional code space are used. The functions affected are ATN, COS, EXP, LOG, SIN, SQR, and TAN.

Note

All switch numbers may be specified as decimal, octal (preceded by &O), or hexadecimal (preceded by &H).

Sample GW-BASIC command lines are as follows:

The following uses 64K bytes of memory and three files; loads and executes the program file *payroll.bas*:

```
A>gwbasic PAYROLL
```

The following uses 64K bytes of memory and six files; loads and executes the program file *invent.bas*:

```
A>gwbasic INVENT /F:6
```

The following disables RS-232 support and uses only the first 32K bytes of memory. 32K bytes above that are reserved for user programs:

```
A>gwbasic /C:0 /M:32768,4096
```

The following uses four files and allows a maximum record length of 512 bytes:

```
A>gwbasic /F:4 /S:512
```

The following uses 64K bytes of memory and three files. Allocates 512 bytes to RS-232 receive buffers and 128 bytes to transmit buffers, and loads and executes the program file *tty.bas*:

```
A>gwbasic TTY /C:512
```

For more information about RS-232 Communications, see Appendix F.

Redirection of Standard Input and Output

When redirected, all INPUT, LINE INPUT, INPUT$, and INKEY$ statements are read from the specified input file instead of the keyboard.

All PRINT statements write to the specified output file instead of the screen.

Error messages go to standard output and to the screen.

File input from KYBD: is still read from the keyboard.

File output to SCRN: still outputs to the screen.

GW-BASIC continues to trap keys when the ON KEY *n* statement is used.

Typing CTRL-BREAK when output is redirected causes GW-BASIC to close any open files, issue the message "Break in line *nnnn*" to standard output, exit GW-BASIC, and return to MS-DOS.

When input is redirected, GW-BASIC continues to read from this source until a CTRL-Z is detected. This condition can be tested with the end-of-file (EOF) function. If the file is not terminated by a CTRL-Z, or if a GW-BASIC file input statement tries to read past the end of file, then any open files are closed, and GW-BASIC returns to MS-DOS.

For further information about these statements and other statements, functions, commands, and variables mentioned in this text, refer to the *GW-BASIC User's Reference*.

Some examples of redirection follow.

```
GWBASIC MYPROG >DATA.OUT
```

Data read by the INPUT and LINE INPUT statements continues to come from the keyboard. Data output by the PRINT statement goes into the *data.out* file.

```
gwbasic MYPROG <DATA.IN
```

Data read by the INPUT and LINE INPUT statements comes from *data.in*. Data output by PRINT continues to go to the screen.

```
gwbasic MYPROG <MYINPUT.DAT >MYOUTPUT.DAT
```

Data read by the INPUT and LINE INPUT statements now comes from the file *myinput.dat*, and data output by the PRINT statements goes into *myoutput.dat*.

```
gwbasic MYPROG <\SALES\JOHN\TRANS.DAT >>\SALES\SALES.DAT
```

Data read by the INPUT and LINE INPUT statements now comes from the file *\sales\john\trans.dat*. Data output by the PRINT statement is appended to the file *\sales\sales.dat*.

2.4 GW-BASIC Statements, Functions, Commands, and Variables

A GW-BASIC program is made up of several elements: keywords, commands, statements, functions, and variables.

2.4.1 Keywords

GW-BASIC keywords, such as **print**, **goto**, and **return** have special significance for the GW-BASIC Interpreter. GW-BASIC interprets keywords as part of statements or commands.

Keywords are also called *reserved words*. They cannot be used as variable names, or the system will interpret them as commands. However, keywords may be embedded within variable names.

Keywords are stored in the system as *tokens* (1- or 2-byte characters) for the most efficient use of memory space.

2.4.2 Commands

Commands and statements are both executable instructions. The difference between commands and statements is that commands are generally executed in the direct mode, or command level of the interpreter. They usually perform some type of program maintenance such as editing, loading, or saving programs. When GW-BASIC is invoked and the GW-BASIC prompt, *Ok*, appears, the system assumes command level.

2.4.3 Statements

A statement, such as ON ERROR...GOTO, is a group of GW-BASIC keywords generally used in GW-BASIC program lines as part of a program. When the program is run, statements are executed when, and as, they appear.

2.4.4 Functions

The GW-BASIC Interpreter performs both numeric and string functions.

2.4.4.1 Numeric Functions

The GW-BASIC Interpreter can perform certain mathematical (arithmetical or algebraic) calculations. For example, it calculates the sine (**sin**), cosine (**cos**), or tangent (**tan**) of angle x.

Unless otherwise indicated, only integer and single-precision results are returned by numeric functions.

2.4.4.2 String Functions

String functions operate on strings. For example, TIME$ and DATE$ return the time and date known by the system. If the current time and date are entered during system start-up, the correct time and date are given (the internal clock in the computer keeps track).

2.4.4.3 User-Defined Functions

Functions can be user-defined by means of the DEF FN statement. These functions can be either string or numeric.

2.4.5 Variables

Certain groups of alphanumeric characters are assigned values and are called *variables*. When variables are built into the GW-BASIC program they provide information as they are executed.

For example, ERR defines the latest error which occurred in the program; ERL gives the location of that error. Variables can also be defined and/or redefined by the user or by program content.

All GW-BASIC commands, statements, functions, and variables are individually described in the *GW-BASIC User's Reference*.

2.5 Line Format

Each of the elements of GW-BASIC can make up sections of a program that are called *statements*. These statements are very similar to sentences in English. Statements are then put together in a logical manner to create programs. The *GW-BASIC User's Reference* describes all of the statements available for use in GW-BASIC.

In a GW-BASIC program, lines have the following format:

nnnnn statement[*statements*]

nnnnn is a line number.

statement is a GW-BASIC statement.

A GW-BASIC program line always begins with a line number and must contain at least one character, but no more than 255 characters. Line numbers indicate the order in which the program lines are stored in memory, and are also used as references when branching and editing. The program line ends when you press the RETURN key.

Depending on the logic of your program, there may be more than one statement on a line. If so, each must be separated by a colon (:). Each of the lines in a program should be preceded by a line number. This number may be any whole integer from 0 to 65529. It is customary to use line numbers such as 10, 20, 30, and 40, in order to leave room for any additional lines that you may wish to include later. Since the computer will run the statements in numerical order, additional lines needn't appear in consecutive order on the screen: for example, if you entered line 35 after line 60, the computer would still run line 35 after line 30 and before line 40. This technique may save your reentering an entire program in order to include one line that you have forgotten.

The width of your screen is 80 characters. If your statement exceeds this width, the cursor will wrap to the next screen line automatically. Only when you press the RETURN key will the computer acknowledge the end of the line. Resist the temptation to press RETURN as you approach the edge of the screen (or beyond). The computer will automatically wrap the line for you. You can also press CTRL-RETURN, which causes the cursor to move to the beginning of the next screen line without actually entering the line. When you press RETURN, the entire logical line is passed to GW-BASIC for storage in the program.

In GW-BASIC, any line of text that begins with a numeric character is considered a program line and is processed in one of three ways after the RETURN key is pressed:

- A new line is added to the program. This occurs if the line number is legal (within the range of 0 through 65529), and if at least one alpha or special character follows the line number in the line.

- An existing line is modified. This occurs if the line number matches the line number of an existing line in the program. The existing line is replaced with the text of the newly-entered line. This process is called *editing*.

Note

Reuse of an existing line number causes all of the information contained in the original line to be lost. Be careful when entering numbers in the indirect mode. You may erase some program lines by accident.

- An existing line is deleted. This occurs if the line number matches the line number of an existing line, and the entered line contains only a line number. If an attempt is made to delete a nonexistent line, an "Undefined line number" error message is displayed.

2.6 Returning to MS-DOS

Before you return to MS-DOS, you must save the work you have entered under GW-BASIC, or the work will be lost.

To return to MS-DOS, type the following after the *Ok* prompt, and press RETURN:

```
system
```

The system returns to MS-DOS, and the *A>* prompt appears on your screen.

Chapter 3
Reviewing and Practicing GW-BASIC

The practice sessions in this chapter will help you review what you have learned. If you have not done so, this is a good time to turn on your computer and load the GW-BASIC Interpreter.

3.1   Example for the Direct Mode

You can use your computer in the direct mode to perform fundamental arithmetic operations. GW-BASIC recognizes the following symbols as arithmetic operators:

Operation	GW-BASIC Operator
Addition	+
Subtraction	-
Multiplication	*
Division	/

To enter a problem, respond to the *Ok* prompt with a question mark (?), followed by the statement of the problem you want to solve, and press the RETURN key. In GW-BASIC, the question mark can be used interchangeably with the keyword PRINT. The answer is then displayed.

Type the following and press the RETURN key:

```
?2+2
```

GW-BASIC will display the answer on your screen:

```
?2+2
4
Ok
```

To practice other arithmetic operations, replace the + sign with the desired operator.

The GW-BASIC language is not restricted to arithmetic functions. You can also enter complex algebraic and trigonometric functions. The formats for these functions are provided in Chapter 6, "Constants, Variables, Expressions and Operators."

3.2   Examples for the Indirect Mode

The GW-BASIC language can be used for functions other than simple algebraic calculations. You can create a program that performs a series of operations and then displays the answer. To begin programming, you create lines of instructions called *statements*. Remember that there can be more than one statement on a line, and that each line is preceded by a number.

For example, to create the command PRINT 2 + 3 as a statement, type the following:

```
10 print 2+3
```

When you press the RETURN key, the cursor shifts to the next line, but nothing else happens. To make the computer perform the calculation, type the following and press the RETURN key:

```
run
```

Your screen should look like this:

```
Ok
10 print 2+3
run
 5
Ok
```

You have just written a program in GW-BASIC.

The computer reserves its calculation until specifically commanded to continue (with the RUN command). This allows you to enter more lines of instruction. When you type the RUN command, the computer does the addition and displays the answer.

The following program has two lines of instructions. Type it in:

```
10 x=3
20 print 2+x
```

Now use the RUN command to have the computer calculate the answer.

Your screen should look like this:

```
Ok
10  x=3
20  print 2+x
run
 5
Ok
```

The two features that distinguish a program from a calculation are

1. the numbered lines
2. the use of the RUN command

These features let the computer know that all the statements have been typed and the computation can be carried out from beginning to end. It is the numbering of the lines that first signals the computer that this is a program, not a calculation, and that it must not do the actual computation until the RUN command is entered.

In other words, calculations are done under the direct mode. Programs are written under the indirect mode.

To display the entire program again, type the LIST command and press the RETURN key:

```
list
```

Your screen should look like this:

```
Ok
10  x=3
20  print 2+x
run
Ok
 5
Ok
list
10  X=3
20  PRINT 2+X
Ok
```

You'll notice a slight change in the program. The lowercase letters you entered have been converted into uppercase letters. The LIST command makes this change automatically.

3.3   Function Keys

Function keys are keys that have been assigned to frequently-used commands. The ten function keys are located on the left side of your keyboard.
A guide to these keys and their assigned commands appears on the bottom
of the GW-BASIC screen. To save time and keystrokes, you can press a function key instead of typing a command name.

For example, to list your program again, you needn't type the LIST command; you can use the function key assigned to it, instead:

1.   Press the F1 key.

2.   Press RETURN.

Your program should appear on the screen.

To run the program, simply press the F2 key, which is assigned to the RUN
command.

As you learn more commands, you'll learn how to use keys F3 through F10.
Chapter 4, "The GW-BASIC Screen Editor," contains more information about
keys used in GW-BASIC.

3.4   Editing Lines

There are two basic ways to change lines. You can

●   delete and replace them

●   alter them with the EDIT command

To delete a line, simply type the line number and press the RETURN key.
For example, if you type *12* and press the RETURN key, line number 12 is
deleted from your program.

To use the EDIT command, type the command EDIT, followed by the
number of the line you want to change. For example, type the following
and press the RETURN key:

```
edit 10
```

You can then use the following keys to perform editing:

Key	Function
CURSOR UP CURSOR DOWN CURSOR LEFT CURSOR RIGHT	Moves the cursor within the statement
BACKSPACE	Deletes the character to the left of the cursor
DELETE (DEL)	Deletes the current character
INSERT (INS)	Lets you insert characters to the left of the cursor

For example, to modify statement (line) 10 to read $x=4$, use the cursor-right control key to move the cursor under the 3, and then type a 4. The number 4 replaces the number 3 in the statement.

Now press the RETURN key, and then the F2 key.

Your screen displays the following:

```
Ok
10  X=4
RUN
 6
Ok
```

3.5 Saving Your Program File

Creating a program is like creating a data file. The program is a file that contains specific instructions, or statements, for the computer. In order to use the program again, you must save it, just as you would a data file.

To save a file in GW-BASIC, use the following procedure:

1. Press the F4 key.

    The command *SAVE "* appears on your screen.

2. Type a name for the program, and press the RETURN key. The file is saved under the name you specified.

To recall a saved file, use the following procedure:

1. Press the F3 key.

   The command *LOAD* " appears on your screen.

2. Type the name of the file.

3. Press RETURN.

The file is loaded into memory, and ready for you to list, edit, or run.

Chapter 4
The GW-BASIC Screen Editor

You can edit GW-BASIC program lines as you enter them, or after they have been saved in a program file.

4.1 Editing Lines in New Files

If an incorrect character is entered as a line is being typed, it can be deleted with the BACKSPACE or DEL keys, or with CTRL-H. After the character is deleted, you can continue to type on the line.

The ESC key lets you delete a line that is in the process of being typed. In other words, if you have not pressed the RETURN key, and you wish to delete the current line of entry, press the ESC key.

To delete the entire program currently residing in memory, enter the NEW command. NEW is usually used to clear memory prior to entering a new program.

4.2 Editing Lines in Saved Files

After you have entered your GW-BASIC program and saved it, you may discover that you need to make some changes. To make these modifications, use the LIST statement to display the program lines that are affected:

1. Reload the program.
2. Type the LIST command, or press the F1 key.
3. Type the line number, or range of numbers, to be edited.

The lines will appear on your screen.

4.2.1 Editing the Information in a Program Line

You can make changes to the information in a line by positioning the cursor where the change is to be made, and by doing one of the following:

- Typing over the characters that are already there.

- Deleting characters to the left of the cursor, using the BACKSPACE key.

- Deleting characters at the cursor position using the DEL key on the number pad.

- Inserting characters at the cursor position by pressing the INS key on the number pad. This moves the characters following the cursor to the right making room for the new information.

- Adding to or truncating characters at the end of the program line.

If you have changed more than one line, be sure to press RETURN on each modified line. The modified lines will be stored in the proper numerical sequence, even if the lines are not updated in numerical order.

Note

A program line will not actually have changes recorded within the GW-BASIC program until the RETURN key is pressed with the cursor positioned somewhere on the edited line.

You do not have to move the cursor to the end of the line before pressing the RETURN key. The GW-BASIC Interpreter remembers where each line ends, and transfers the whole line, even if RETURN is pressed while the cursor is located in the middle or at the beginning of the line.

To truncate, or cut off, a line at the current cursor position, type CTRL-END or CTRL-E, followed by pressing the RETURN key.

If you have originally saved your program to a program file, make sure that you save the edited version of your program. If you do not do this, your modifications will not be recorded.

4.3 Special Keys

The GW-BASIC Interpreter recognizes nine of the numeric keys on the right side of your keyboard. It also recognizes the BACKSPACE key, ESC key, and the CTRL key. The following keys and key sequences have special functions in GW-BASIC:

Key	**Function**
BACKSPACE or CTRL-H	Deletes the last character typed, or deletes the character to the left of the cursor. All characters to the right of the cursor are moved left one position. Subsequent characters and lines within the current logical line are moved up as with the DEL key.
CTRL-BREAK or CTRL-C	Returns to the direct mode, without saving changes made to the current line. It will also exit auto line-numbering mode.
CTRL-CURSOR-LEFT or CTRL-B	Moves the cursor to the beginning of the previous word. The previous word is defined as the next character to the left of the cursor in the set A to Z or in the set 0 to 9.
CTRL-CURSOR-RIGHT or CTRL-F	Moves the cursor to the beginning of the next word. The next word is defined as the next character to the right of the cursor in the set A to Z or in the set 0 to 9. In other words, the cursor moves to the next number or letter after a blank or other special character.
CURSOR-DOWN or CTRL-–	Moves the cursor down one line on the screen.
CURSOR-LEFT or CTRL-]	Moves the cursor one position left. When the cursor is advanced beyond the left edge of the screen, it will wrap to the right side of the screen on the preceding line.
CURSOR-RIGHT or CTRL-\	Moves the cursor one position right. When the cursor is advanced beyond the right edge of the screen, it will wrap to the left side of the screen on the following line.
CURSOR-UP or CTRL-6	Moves the cursor up one line on the screen.
CTRL-BACKSPACE or DEL	Deletes the character positioned over the cursor. All characters to the right of the one deleted are then moved one position left to fill in where the deletion was made.
	If a logical line extends beyond one physical line, characters on subsequent lines are moved left one position to fill in the previous space, and the character in the first column of each subsequent line is moved up to the end of the preceding line.

DEL (delete) is the opposite of INS (insert). Deleting text reduces logical line length.

CTRL-END or CTRL-E	Erases from the cursor position to the end of the logical line. All physical screen lines are erased until the terminating RETURN is found.
CTRL-N or END	Moves the cursor to the end of the logical line. Characters typed from this position are added to the line.
CTRL-RETURN or CTRL-J	Moves the cursor to the beginning of the next screen line. This lets you create logical program lines which are longer than the physical screen width. Logical lines may be up to 255 characters long. This function may also be used as a line feed.
CTRL-M or RETURN	Enters a line into the GW-BASIC program. It also moves the cursor to the next logical line.
CTRL-[or ESC	Erases the entire logical line on which the cursor is located.
CTRL-G	Causes a beep to emit from your computer's speaker.
CTRL-K or HOME	Moves the cursor to the upper left corner of the screen. The screen contents are unchanged.
CTRL-HOME or CTRL-L	Clears the screen and positions the cursor in the upper left corner of the screen.
CTRL-R or INS	Turns the Insert Mode on and off.

Insert Mode is indicated by the cursor blotting the lower half of the character position. In Graphics Mode, the normal cursor covers the whole character position. When Insert Mode is active, only the lower half of the character position is blanked by the cursor.

When Insert Mode is off, characters typed replace existing characters on the line. The SPACEBAR erases the character at the current cursor position and moves the cursor one character to the right. The CURSOR-RIGHT key moves the cursor one character to the right, but does not delete the character.

When Insert Mode is off, pressing the TAB key moves the cursor over characters until the next tab stop is reached. Tab stops occur every eight character positions.

When Insert Mode is on, characters following the cursor are moved to the right as typed characters are inserted before them at the current cursor position. After each keystroke, the cursor moves one position to the right. Line wrapping is observed. That is, as characters move off the right side of the screen, they are inserted from the left on subsequent lines. Insertions increase logical line length.

When Insert Mode is on, pressing the TAB key causes blanks to be inserted from current cursor position to the next tab stop. Line wrapping is observed as above.

CTRL-NUM LOCK or CTRL-S	Places the computer in a pause state. To resume operation, press any other key.
CTRL-PRTSC	Causes characters printed on the screen to echo to the lineprinter (**lpt1:**). In other words, you will be printing what you type on the screen. Pressing CTRL-PRTSC a second time turns off the echoing of characters to **lpt1:**.
SHIFT-PRTSC	Sends the current screen contents to the printer, effectively creating a snapshot of the screen.
CTRL-I or TAB	Moves the cursor to the next tab stop. Tab stops occur every eight columns.

4.4 Function Keys

Certain keys or combinations of keys let you perform frequently-used commands or functions with a minimum number of keystrokes. These keys are called *function keys*.

The special function keys that appear on the left side of your keyboard can be temporarily redefined to meet the programming requirements and specific functions that your program may require.

Function keys allow rapid entry of as many as 15 characters into a program with one keystroke. These keys are located on the left side of your keyboard and are labelled F1 through F10. GW-BASIC has already assigned special functions to each of these keys. You will notice that after you load GW-BASIC, these special key functions appear on the bottom line of your screen. These key assignments have been selected for you as some of the most frequently used commands.

Initially, the function keys are assigned the following special functions:

Table 4.1

GW-BASIC Function Key Assignments

Key	Function	Key	Function
F1	LIST	F6	,"LPT1:"<-
F2	RUN<-	F7	TRON<-
F3	LOAD"	F8	TROFF<-
F4	SAVE"	F9	KEY
F5	CONT<-	F10	SCREEN 0,0,0<-

Note

The <- following a function indicates that you needn't press the RETURN key after the function key. The selected command will be immediately executed.

If you choose, you may change the assignments of these keys. Any one or all of the 10 function keys may be redefined. For more information, see the KEY and ON KEY statements in the *GW-BASIC User's Reference*.

Chapter 5
Creating and Using Files

There are two types of files in MS-DOS systems:

- *Program files*, which contain the program or instructions for the computer

- *Data files*, which contain information used or created by program files

5.1 Program File Commands

The following are the commands and statements most frequently used with program files. The *GW-BASIC User's Reference* contains more information on each of them.

SAVE *filename*[,**a**][,**p**]

Writes to diskette the program currently residing in memory.

LOAD *filename*[,**r**]

Loads the program from a diskette into memory. LOAD deletes the current contents of memory and closes all files before loading the program.

RUN *filename*[,**r**]

Loads the program from a diskette into memory and runs it immediately. RUN deletes the current contents of memory and closes all files before loading the program.

MERGE *filename*

Loads the program from a diskette into memory, but does not delete the current program already in memory.

KILL *filename*

Deletes the file from a diskette. This command can also be used with data files.

NAME *old filename* **AS** *new filename*

Changes the name of a diskette file. Only the *name* of the file is changed. The file is not modified, and it remains in the same space and position on the disk. This command can also be used with data files.

5.2   Data Files

GW-BASIC programs can work with two types of data files:

- Sequential files
- Random access files

Sequential files are easier to create than random access files, but are limited in flexibility and speed when accessing data. Data written to a sequential file is a series of ASCII characters. Data is stored, one item after another (sequentially), in the order sent. Data is read back in the same way.

Creating and accessing random access files requires more program steps than sequential files, but random files require less room on the disk, because GW-BASIC stores them in a compressed format in the form of a string.

The following sections discuss how to create and use these two types of data files.

5.2.1   Creating a Sequential File

The following statements and functions are used with sequential files:

CLOSE	LOF
EOF	OPEN
INPUT#	PRINT#
LINE INPUT#	PRINT# USING
LOC	UNLOCK
LOCK	WRITE#

The following program steps are required to create a sequential file and access the data in the file:

1. Open the file in output (O) mode. The current program will use this file first for output:

    OPEN "O",#1,"*filename*"

2. Write data to the file using the PRINT# or WRITE# statement:

    PRINT#1,A$
    PRINT#1,B$
    PRINT#1,C$

3. To access the data in the file, you must close the file and reopen it in input (I) mode:

    CLOSE #1
    OPEN "I",#1,"filename"

4. Use the INPUT# or LINE INPUT# statement to read data from the sequential file into the program:

    INPUT#1,X$,Y$,Z$

Example 1 is a short program that creates a sequential file, *data*, from information input at the terminal.

Example 1

```
10  OPEN "O",#1,"DATA"
20  INPUT "NAME";N$
30  IF N$="DONE" THEN END
40  INPUT "DEPARTMENT";D$
50  INPUT "DATE HIRED";H$
60  PRINT#1,N$;",",D$",";H$
70  PRINT:GOTO 20
RUN
NAME? MICKEY MOUSE
DEPARTMENT? AUDIO/VISUAL AIDS
DATE HIRED? 01/12/72

NAME? SHERLOCK HOLMES
DEPARTMENT? RESEARCH
DATE HIRED? 12/03/65

NAME? EBENEEZER SCROOGE
DEPARTMENT? ACCOUNTING
DATE HIRED? 04/27/78

NAME? SUPER MANN
DEPARTMENT? MAINTENANCE
DATE HIRED? 08/16/78

NAME? DONE
OK
```

5.2.2   Accessing a Sequential File

The program in Example 2 accesses the file *data*, created in the program in Example 1, and displays the name of everyone hired in 1978.

Example 2

```
10  OPEN "I",#1,"DATA"
20  INPUT#1,N$,D$,H$
30  IF RIGHT$(H$,2)="78" THEN PRINT N$
40  GOTO 20
50  CLOSE #1
RUN
EBENEEZER SCROOGE
SUPER MANN
Input past end in 20
Ok
```

The program in Example 2 reads, sequentially, every item in the file. When all the data has been read, line 20 causes an "Input past end" error. To avoid this error, insert line 15, which uses the EOF function to test for end of file:

```
15  IF EOF(1) THEN END
```

and change line 40 to GOTO 15.

A program that creates a sequential file can also write formatted data to the diskette with the PRINT# USING statement. For example, the following statement could be used to write numeric data to diskette without explicit delimiters:

```
PRINT#1,USING"####.##,";A,B,C,D
```

The comma at the end of the format string serves to separate the items in the disk file.

The LOC function, when used with a sequential file, returns the number of 128-byte records that have been written to or read from the file since it was opened.

5.2.3 Adding Data to a Sequential File

When a sequential file is opened in O mode, the current contents are destroyed. To add data to an existing file without destroying its contents, open the file in append (A) mode.

The program in Example 3 can be used to create, or to add onto a file called *names*. This program illustrates the use of LINE INPUT. LINE INPUT will read in characters until it sees a carriage return indicator, or until it has read 255 characters. It does not stop at quotation marks or commas.

Example 3

```
10 ON ERROR GOTO 2000
20 OPEN "A",#1,"NAMES"
110 REM ADD NEW ENTRIES TO FILE
120 INPUT "NAME";N$
130 IF N$="" THEN 200 'CARRIAGE RETURN EXITS INPUT LOOP
140 LINE INPUT "ADDRESS? ";A$
150 LINE INPUT "BIRTHDAY? ";B$
160 PRINT#1,N$
170 PRINT#1,A$
180 PRINT#1,B$
190 PRINT:GOTO 120
200 CLOSE #1
2000 ON ERROR GOTO 0
```

In lines 10 and 2000 the ON ERROR GOTO statement is being used. This statement enables error trapping and specifies the first line (2000) of the error handling subroutine. Line 10 enables the error handling routine. Line 2000 disables the error handling routine and is the point where GW-BASIC branches to print the error messages.

5.3 Random Access Files

Information in random access files is stored and accessed in distinct, numbered units called *records*. Since the information is called by number, the data can be called from any disk location; the program needn't read the entire disk, as when seeking sequential files, to locate data. GW-BASIC supports large random files. The maximum logical record number is $2^{32} - 1$.

The following statements and functions are used with random files:

CLOSE	FIELD	MKI$
CVD	LOC	MKS$
CVI	LOCK	OPEN
CVS	LOF	PUT
EOF	LSET/RSET	UNLOCK
ET	MKD$	

5.3.1 Creating a Random Access File

The following program steps are required to create a random data file:

1. Open the file for random access (R) mode. The following example specifies a record length of 32 bytes. If the record length is omitted, the default is 128 bytes.

   OPEN "R",#1,"*filename*",32

2. Use the FIELD statement to allocate space in the random buffer for the variables that will be written to the random file:

   FIELD#1,20 AS N$,4 AS A$,8 AS P$

   In this example, the first 20 positions (bytes) in the random file buffer are allocated to the string variable N$. The next 4 positions are allocated to A$; the next 8 to P$.

3. Use LSET or RSET to move the data into the random buffer fields in left- or right-justified format (L = left SET; R = right SET). Numeric values must be made into strings when placed in the buffer. MKI$ converts an integer value into a string, MKS$ converts a single-precision value, and MKD$ converts a double-precision value.

   LSET N$ = X$
   LSET A$ = MKS$(AMT)
   LSET P$ = TEL$

4. Write the data from the buffer to the diskette using the PUT statement:

   PUT #1,CODE%

The program in Example 4 takes information keyed as input at the terminal and writes it to a random access data file. Each time the PUT statement is executed, a record is written to the file. In the example, the 2-digit CODE% input in line 30 becomes the record number.

Note

Do not use a fielded string variable in an INPUT or LET statement. This causes the pointer for that variable to point into string space instead of the random file buffer.

Example 4

```
10  OPEN "R",#1,"INFOFILE",32
20  FIELD#1,20 AS N$, 4 AS A$, 8 AS P$
30  INPUT "2-DIGIT CODE";CODE%
40  INPUT "NAME";X$
50  INPUT "AMOUNT";AMT
60  INPUT "PHONE";TEL$:PRINT
70  LSET N$=X$
80  LSET A$=MKS$(AMT)
90  LSET P$=TEL$
100 PUT #1,CODE%
110 GOTO 30
```

5.3.2   Accessing a Random Access File

The following program steps are required to access a random file:

1. Open the file in R mode:

    OPEN "R",#1,*filename*,32

2. Use the FIELD statement to allocate space in the random buffer for the variables that will be read from the file:

    FIELD, #1, 20 AS N$, 4 AS A$, 8 AS P$

    In this example, the first 20 positions (bytes) in the random file buffer are allocated to the string variable N$. The next 4 positions are allocated to A$; the next 8 to P$.

Note

In a program that performs both INPUT and OUTPUT on the same random file, you can often use just one OPEN statement and one FIELD statement.

3. Use the GET statement to move the desired record into the random buffer:

GET #1,CODE%

The data in the buffer can now be accessed by the program.

4. Convert numeric values back to numbers using the convert functions: CVI for integers, CVS for single-precision values, and CVD for double-precision values.

```
PRINT N$
PRINT CVS(A$)
       .
       .
       .
```

The program in Example 5 accesses the random file, *infofile*, that was created in Example 4. By inputting the 3-digit code, the information associated with that code is read from the file and displayed.

Example 5

```
10 OPEN "R",#1,"INFOFILE",32
20 FIELD #1, 20 AS N$, 4 AS A$, 8 AS P$
30 INPUT "2-DIGIT CODE";CODE%
40 GET #1, CODE%
50 PRINT N$
60 PRINT USING "$$###.##";CVS(A$)
70 PRINT P$:PRINT
80 GOTO 30
```

With random files, the LOC function returns the current record number. The current record number is the last record number used in a GET or PUT statement. For example, the following line ends program execution if the current record number in file#1 is higher than 99:

```
IF LOC(1)#99 THEN END
```

Example 6 is an inventory program that illustrates random file access. In this program, the record number is used as the part number, and it is assumed that the inventory will contain no more than 100 different part numbers.

Lines 900-960 initialize the data file by writing CHR$(255) as the first character of each record. This is used later (line 270 and line 500) to determine whether an entry already exists for that part number.

Lines 130-220 display the different inventory functions that the program performs. When you type in the desired function number, line 230 branches to the appropriate subroutine.

Example 6

```
120 OPEN"R",#1,"INVEN.DAT",39
125 FIELD#1,1 AS F$,30 AS D$, 2 AS Q$,2 AS R$,4 AS P$
130 PRINT:PRINT "FUNCTIONS:":PRINT
135 PRINT 1,"INITIALIZE FILE"
140 PRINT 2,"CREATE A NEW ENTRY"
150 PRINT 3,"DISPLAY INVENTORY FOR ONE PART"
160 PRINT 4,"ADD TO STOCK"
170 PRINT 5,"SUBTRACT FROM STOCK"
180 PRINT 6,"DISPLAY ALL ITEMS BELOW REORDER LEVEL"
220 PRINT:PRINT:INPUT"FUNCTION";FUNCTION
225 IF (FUNCTION<1)OR(FUNCTION>6) THEN PRINT "BAD FUNCTION
NUMBER":GOTO 130
230 ON FUNCTION GOSUB 900,250,390,480,560,680
240 GOTO 220
250 REM BUILD NEW ENTRY
260 GOSUB 840
270 IF ASC(F$) < > 255 THEN INPUT"OVERWRITE";A$:
 IF A$ < > "Y" THEN RETURN
280 LSET F$=CHR$(0)
290 INPUT "DESCRIPTION";DESC$
300 LSET D$=DESC$
310 INPUT "QUANTITY IN STOCK";Q%
320 LSET Q$=MKI$(Q%)
330 INPUT "REORDER LEVEL";R%
340 LSET R$=MKI$(R%)
350 INPUT "UNIT PRICE";P
360 LSET P$=MKS$(P)
370 PUT#1,PART%
380 RETURN
390 REM DISPLAY ENTRY
400 GOSUB 840
410 IF ASC(F$)=255 THEN PRINT "NULL ENTRY":RETURN
420 PRINT USING "PART NUMBER ###";PART%
430 PRINT D$
440 PRINT USING "QUANTITY ON HAND #####";CVI(Q$)
450 PRINT USING "REORDER LEVEL #####";CVI(R$)
460 PRINT USING "UNIT PRICE $$##.##";CVS(P$)
470 RETURN
480 REM ADD TO STOCK
490 GOSUB 840
500 IF ASC(F$)=255 THEN PRINT "NULL ENTRY":RETURN
510 PRINT D$:INPUT "QUANTITY TO ADD";A%
```

```
520 Q%=CVI(Q$)+A%
530 LSET Q$=MKI$(Q%)
540 PUT#1,PART%
550 RETURN
560 REM REMOVE FROM STOCK
570 GOSUB 840
580 IF ASC(F$)=255 THEN PRINT "NULL ENTRY":RETURN
590 PRINT D$
600 INPUT "QUANTITY TO SUBTRACT";S%
610 Q%=CVI(Q$)
620 IF (Q%-S%)<0 THEN PRINT "ONLY";Q%;" IN STOCK" :GOTO 600
630 Q%=Q%-S%
640 IF Q%= < CVI(R$) THEN PRINT "QUANTITY NOW";Q%;
"REORDER LEVEL";CVI(R$)
650 LSET Q$=MKI$(Q%)
660 PUT#1,PART%
670 RETURN
680 REM DISPLAY ITEMS BELOW REORDER LEVEL4
690 FOR I=1 TO 100
710 GET#1,I
720 IF CVI(Q$)<CVI(R$) THEN PRINT D$;" QUANTITY";
CVI(Q$) TAB(50) "REORDER LEVEL";CVI(R$)
730 NEXT I
740 RETURN
840 INPUT "PART NUMBER";PART%
850 IF(PART% < 1)OR(PART% > 100) THEN PRINT "BAD PART NUMBER":
GOTO 840 ELSE GET#1,PART%:RETURN
890 END
900 REM INITIALIZE FILE
910 INPUT "ARE YOU SURE";B$:IF B$ < > "Y" THEN RETURN
920 LSET F$=CHR$(255)
930 FOR I=1 TO 100
940 PUT#1,I
950 NEXT I
960 RETURN
```

Chapter 6
Constants, Variables, Expressions and Operators

After you have learned the fundamentals of programming in GW-BASIC, you will find that you will want to write more complex programs. The information in this chapter will help you learn more about the use of constants, variables, expressions, and operators in GW-BASIC, and how they can be used to develop more sophisticated programs.

6.1 Constants

Constants are static values the GW-BASIC Interpreter uses during execution of your program. There are two types of constants: *string* and *numeric*.

A *string constant* is a sequence of 0 to 255 alphanumeric characters enclosed in double quotation marks. The following are sample string constants:

"HELLO"
"$25,000.00"
"Number of Employees"

Numeric constants can be positive or negative. When entering a numeric constant in GW-BASIC, you should not type the commas. For instance, if the number *10,000* were to be entered as a constant, it would be typed as *10000*. There are five types of numeric constants: *integer*, *fixed-point*, *floating-point*, *hexadecimal*, and *octal*.

Constant	Description
Integer	Whole numbers between -32768 and $+32767$. They do not contain decimal points.
Fixed-Point	Positive or negative real numbers that contain decimal points.
Floating-Point Constants	Positive or negative numbers represented in exponential form (similar to scientific notation). A floating-point constant consists of an optionally-signed integer or fixed-point number (the mantissa), followed by the letter E and an optionally-signed integer (the exponent).

The allowable range for floating-point constants is 3.0×10^{-39} to 1.7×10^{38}. For example:

235.988E-7 = .0000235988
2359E6 = 2359000000

Hexadecimal
: Hexadecimal numbers with prefix &H. For example:

&H76
&H32F

Octal
: Octal numbers with the prefix &O or &. For example:

&O347
&1234

6.1.1 Single- and Double-Precision Form for Numeric Constants

Numeric constants can be integers, single-precision or double-precision numbers. Integer constants are stored as whole numbers only. Single-precision numeric constants are stored with 7 digits (although only 6 may be accurate). Double-precision numeric constants are stored with 17 digits of precision, and printed with as many as 16 digits.

A single-precision constant is any numeric constant with either

- seven or fewer digits
- exponential form using E
- a trailing exclamation point (!)

A double-precision constant is any numeric constant with either

- eight or more digits
- exponential form using D
- a trailing number sign (#)

The following are examples of single- and double-precision numeric constants:

Single-Precision Constants	Double-Precision Constants
46.8	345692811
− 1.09E-06	− 1.09432D-06
3489.0	3490.0#
22.5!	7654321.1234

6.2   Variables

Variables are the names that you have chosen to represent values used in a GW-BASIC program. The value of a variable may be assigned specifically, or may be the result of calculations in your program. If a variable is assigned no value, GW-BASIC assumes the variable's value to be zero.

6.2.1   Variable Names and Declarations

GW-BASIC variable names may be any length; up to 40 characters are significant. The characters allowed in a variable name are letters, numbers, and the decimal point. The first character in the variable name must be a letter. Special type declaration characters are also allowed.

Reserved words (all the words used as GW-BASIC commands, statements, functions, and operators) can't be used as variable names. However, if the reserved word is embedded within the variable name, it will be allowed.

Variables may represent either numeric values or strings.

6.2.2   Type Declaration Characters

Type declaration characters indicate what a variable represents. The following type declaration characters are recognized:

Character	Type of Variable
$	String variable
%	Integer variable
!	Single-precision variable
#	Double-precision variable

The following are sample variable names for each type:

Variable Type	Sample Name
String variable	N$
Integer variable	LIMIT%
Single-precision variable	MINIMUM!
Double-precision variable	Pl#

The default type for a numeric variable name is single-precision. Double-precision, while very accurate, uses more memory space and more calculation time. Single-precision is sufficiently accurate for most applications. However, the seventh significant digit (if printed) will not always be accurate. You should be very careful when making conversions between integer, single-precision, and double-precision variables.

The following variable is a single-precision value by default:

ABC

Variables beginning with FN are assumed to be calls to a user-defined function.

The GW-BASIC statements DEFINT, DEFSTR, DEFSNG, and DEFDBL may be included in a program to declare the types of values for certain variable names.

6.2.3 Array Variables

An *array* is a group or table of values referenced by the same variable name. Each element in an array is referenced by an *array variable* that is a subscripted integer or an integer expression. The subscript is enclosed within parentheses. An array variable name has as many subscripts as there are dimensions in the array.

For example,

V(10)

references a value in a one-dimensional array, while

T(1,4)

references a value in a two-dimensional array.

The maximum number of dimensions for an array in GW-BASIC is 255. The maximum number of elements per dimension is 32767.

Note

If you are using an array with a subscript value greater than 10, you should use the DIM statement. Refer to the *GW-BASIC User's Reference* for more information. If a subscript greater than the maximum specified is used, you will receive the error message "Subscript out of range."

Multidimensional arrays (more than one subscript separated by commas) are useful for storing tabular data. For example, A(1,4) could be used to represent a two-row, five-column array such as the following:

Column		0	1	2	3	4
Row	0	10	20	30	40	50
Row	1	60	70	80	90	100

In this example, element A(1,2)=80 and A(0,3)=40.

Rows and columns begin with 0, not 1, unless otherwise declared. For more information, see the OPTION BASE statement in the *GW-BASIC User's Reference*.

6.2.4 Memory Space Requirements for Variable Storage

The different types of variables require different amounts of storage. Depending on the storage and memory capacity of your computer and the size of the program that you are developing, these can be important considerations.

Variable	Required Bytes of Storage
Integer	2
Single-precision	4
Double-precision	8

Arrays	Required Bytes of Storage
Integer	2 per element
Single-precision	4 per element
Double-precision	8 per element

Strings:

Three bytes overhead, plus the present contents of the string as one byte for each character in the string. Quotation marks marking the beginning and end of each string are not counted.

6.3   Type Conversion

When necessary, GW-BASIC converts a numeric constant from one type of variable to another, according to the following rules:

- If a numeric constant of one type is set equal to a numeric variable of a different type, the number is stored as the type declared in the variable name. For example:

```
10 A% = 23.42
20 PRINT A%
RUN
 23
```

   If a string variable is set equal to a numeric value or vice versa, a "Type Mismatch" error occurs.

- During an expression evaluation, all of the operands in an arithmetic or relational operation are converted to the same degree of precision; that is, that of the most precise operand. Also, the result of an arithmetic operation is returned to this degree of precision. For example:

```
10 D# = 6#/7
20 PRINT D#
RUN
 .8571428571428571
```

The arithmetic is performed in double-precision, and the result is returned in D# as a double-precision value.

```
10 D = 6#/7
20 PRINT D
RUN
```

The arithmetic is performed in double-precision, and the result is returned to D (single-precision variable) rounded and printed as a single-precision value.

- Logical operators convert their operands to integers and return an integer result. Operands must be within the range of -32768 to 32767 or an "Overflow" error occurs.

- When a floating-point value is converted to an integer, the fractional portion is rounded. For example:

```
10 C% = 55.88
20 PRINT C%
RUN
 56
```

- If a double-precision variable is assigned a single-precision value, only the first seven digits (rounded) of the converted number are valid. This is because only seven digits of accuracy were supplied with the single-precision value. The absolute value of the difference between the printed double-precision number, and the original single-precision value, is less than 6.3E-8 times the original single-precision value. For example:

```
10 A = 2.04
20 B# = A
30 PRINT A;B#
RUN
 2.04   2.039999961853027
```

6.4   Expressions and Operators

An expression may be simply a string or numeric constant, a variable, or it may combine constants and variables with operators to produce a single value.

Operators perform mathematical or logical operations on values. The operators provided by GW-BASIC are divided into four categories:

- Arithmetic

- Relational

- Logical

- Functional

6.4.1   Arithmetic Operators

The following are the arithmetic operators recognized by GW-BASIC. They appear in order of precedence.

Operator	Operation
^	Exponentiation
-	Negation
*	Multiplication
/	Floating-point Division
+	Addition
-	Subtraction

Operations within parentheses are performed first. Inside the parentheses, the usual order of precedence is maintained.

The following are sample algebraic expressions and their GW-BASIC counterparts:

Algebraic Expression	BASIC Expression
$\dfrac{X-Z}{Y}$	(X-Y)/Z
$\dfrac{XY}{Z}$	X*Y/Z
$\dfrac{X+Y}{Z}$	(X + Y)/Z
$(X^2)^Y$	(X^2)^Y
X^{Y^Z}	X^(Y^Z)
$X(-Y)$	X*(-Y)

Two consecutive operators must be separated by parentheses.

6.4.1.1 Integer Division and Modulus Arithmetic

Two additional arithmetic operators are available: integer division and modulus arithmetic.

Integer division is denoted by the backslash (\). The operands are rounded to integers (must be within the range of -32768 to 32767) before the division is performed, and the quotient is truncated to an integer.

The following are examples of integer division:

```
10\4 = 2

25.68\6.99 = 3
```

In the order of occurrence within GW-BASIC, the integer division will be performed just after floating-point division.

Modulus arithmetic is denoted by the operator MOD. It gives the integer value that is the remainder of an integer division.

The following are examples of modulus arithmetic:

```
10.4 MOD 4 = 2
(10/4=2 with a remainder 2)

25.68 MOD 6.99 = 5
(26/7=3 with a remainder 5)
```

In the order of occurrence within GW-BASIC, modulus arithmetic follows integer division. The INT and FIX functions, described in the *GW-BASIC User's Reference*, are also useful in modulus arithmetic.

6.4.1.2 Overflow and Division by Zero

If, during the evaluation of an expression, a division by zero is encountered, the "Division by zero" error message appears, machine infinity with the sign of the numerator is supplied as the result of the division, and execution continues.

If the evaluation of an exponentiation results in zero being raised to a negative power, the "Division by Zero" error message appears, positive machine infinity is supplied as the result of the exponentiation, and execution continues.

If overflow occurs, the "Overflow" error message appears, machine infinity with the algebraically correct sign is supplied as the result, and execution continues. The errors that occur in overflow and division by zero will not be trapped by the error trapping function.

6.4.2 Relational Operators

Relational operators let you compare two values. The result of the comparison is either true (-1) or false (0). This result can then be used to make a decision regarding program flow.

Table 6.1 displays the relational operators.

Table 6.1

Relational Operators

Operator	Relation Tested	Expression
=	Equality	X = Y
<>	Inequality	X<>Y
<	Less than	X<Y
>	Greater than	X>Y
<=	Less than or equal to	X<=Y
>=	Greater than or equal to	X>=Y

The equal sign is also used to assign a value to a variable. See the LET statement in the *GW-BASIC User's Reference.*

When arithmetic and relational operators are combined in one expression, the arithmetic is always performed first:

```
X+Y  <  (T-1)/Z
```

This expression is true if the value of X plus Y is less than the value of T − 1 divided by Z.

6.4.3 Logical Operators

Logical operators perform tests on multiple relations, bit manipulation, or boolean operations. The logical operator returns a bit-wise result which is either true (not zero) or false (zero). In an expression, logical operations are performed after arithmetic and relational operations. The outcome of a logical operation is determined as shown in the following table. The operators are listed in order of precedence.

Table 6.2

Results Returned by Logical Operations

Operation	Value	Value	Result
NOT	X		NOT X
	T		F
	F		T
AND	X	Y	X AND Y
	T	T	T
	T	F	F
	F	T	F
	F	F	F

Table 6.2 *(continued)*

Operation	Value	Value	Result
OR	X	Y	X OR Y
	T	T	T
	T	F	T
	F	T	T
	F	F	F
XOR	X	Y	X XOR Y
	T	T	F
	T	F	T
	F	T	T
	F	F	F
EQV	X	Y	X EQV Y
	T	T	T
	T	F	F
	F	T	F
	F	F	T
IMP	X	Y	X IMP Y
	T	T	T
	T	F	F
	F	T	T
	F	F	T

Just as the relational operators can be used to make decisions regarding program flow, logical operators can connect two or more relations and return a true or false value to be used in a decision. For example:

```
IF D<200 AND F<4 THEN 80
IF I>10 OR K<0 THEN 50
IF NOT P THEN 100
```

Logical operators convert their operands to 16-bit, signed, two's complement integers within the range of -32768 to $+32767$. If the operands are not within this range, an error results. If both operands are supplied as 0 or

−1, logical operators return 0 or −1. The given operation is performed on these integers in bits; that is, each bit of the result is determined by the corresponding bits in the two operands.

Thus, it is possible to use logical operators to test bytes for a particular bit pattern. For instance, the AND operator may be used to mask all but one of the bits of a status byte at a machine I/O port. The OR operator may be used to merge two bytes to create a particular binary value. The following examples demonstrate how the logical operators work:

Example	Explanation
63 AND 16 = 16	63 = binary 111111 and 16 = binary 10000, so 63 AND 16 = 16
15 AND 14 = 14	15 = binary 1111 and 14 = binary 1110, so 15 AND 14 = 14 (binary 1110)
-1 AND 8 = 8	-1 = binary 1111111111111111 and 8 = binary 1000, so -1 AND 8 = 8
4 OR 2 = 6	4 = binary 100 and 2 = binary 10, so 4 OR 2 = 6 (binary 110)
10 OR 10 = 10	10 = binary 1010, so 1010 OR 1010 = 1010 (10)
-1 OR -2 = -1	-1 = binary 1111111111111111 and -2 = binary 1111111111111110, so -1 OR -2 = -1. The bit complement of 16 zeros is 16 ones, which is the two's complement representation of -1.
NOT X = -(X + 1)	The two's complement of any integer is the bit complement plus one.

6.4.4 Functional Operators

A function is used in an expression to call a predetermined operation that is to be performed on an operand. GW-BASIC has intrinsic functions that reside in the system, such as SQR (square root) or SIN (sine).

GW-BASIC also allows user-defined functions written by the programmer. See the DEF FN statement in the *GW-BASIC User's Reference*.

6.4.5 String Operators

To compare strings, use the same relational operators used with numbers:

Operator	Meaning
=	Equal to
<>	Unequal
<	Less than
>	Greater than
< =	Less than or equal to
> =	Greater than or equal to

The GW-BASIC Interpreter compares strings by taking one character at a time from each string and comparing their ASCII codes. If the ASCII codes in each string are the same, the strings are equal. If the ASCII codes differ, the lower code number will precede the higher code. If the interpreter reaches the end of one string during string comparison, the shorter string is said to be smaller, providing that both strings are the same up to that point. Leading and trailing blanks are significant.

For example:

```
"AA" < "AB"
"FILENAME" = "FILENAME"
"X&" > "X#"
"CL " > "CL"
"kg" > "KG"
"SMYTH" < "SMYTHE"
B$ < "9/12/78" where B$ = "8/12/78"
```

String comparisons can also be used to test string values or to alphabetize strings. All string constants used in comparison expressions must be enclosed in quotation marks.

Strings can be concatenated by using the plus (+) sign. For example:

```
10 A$="FILE":B$="NAME"
20 PRINT A$+B$
30 PRINT "NEW " + A$+B$
RUN
FILENAME
NEW FILENAME
```

GW-BASIC
User's Reference

ABS Function

Purpose:

To return the absolute value of the expression n.

Syntax:

ABS(n)

Comments:

n must be a numeric expression.

Examples:

```
PRINT ABS(7*(-5))
35
Ok
```

Prints 35 as the result of the action.

ASC Function

Purpose:

To return a numeric value that is the ASCII code for the first character of the string x$.

Syntax:

ASC(x$)

Comments:

If x$ is null, an "Illegal Function Call" error is returned.

If x$ begins with an uppercase letter, the value returned will be within the range of 65 to 90.

If x$ begins with a lowercase letter, the range is 97 to 122.

Numbers 0 to 9 return 48 to 57, sequentially.

See the CHR$ function for ASCII-to-string conversion.

See Appendix C in the *GW-BASIC User's Guide* for ASCII codes.

Examples:

```
10 X$="TEN"
20 PRINT ASC(X$)
RUN
        84
Ok
```

84 is the ASCII code for the letter *T*.

ATN Function

Purpose:

To return the arctangent of x, when x is expressed in radians.

Syntax:

ATN(x)

Comments:

The result is within the range of $-\pi/2$ to $\pi/2$.

The expression x may be any numeric type. The evaluation of ATN is performed in single precision unless the **/d** switch is used when GW-BASIC is executed.

To convert from degrees to radians, multiply by $\pi/180$.

Examples:

```
10 INPUT X
20 PRINT ATN(X)
RUN
? 3
1.249046
Ok
```

Prints the arctangent of 3 radians (1.249046).

AUTO Command

Purpose:

To generate and increment line numbers automatically each time you press the RETURN key.

Syntax:

AUTO [*line number*][,[*increment*]]
AUTO .[,[*increment*]]

Comments:

AUTO is useful for program entry because it makes typing line numbers unnecessary.

AUTO begins numbering at *line number* and increments each subsequent line number by *increment*. The default for both values is 10.

The period (.) can be used as a substitute for *line number* to indicate the current line.

If *line number* is followed by a comma, and *increment* is not specified, the last increment specified in an AUTO command is assumed.

If AUTO generates a *line number* that is already being used, an asterisk appears after the number to warn that any input will replace the existing line. However, pressing RETURN immediately after the asterisk saves the line and generates the next line number.

AUTO is terminated by entering CTRL-BREAK or CTRL-C. GW-BASIC will then return to command level.

Note

The line in which CTRL-BREAK or CTRL-C is entered is not saved. To be sure that you save all desired text, use CTRL-BREAK and CTRL-C only on lines by themselves.

Examples:

```
AUTO 100,50
```

Generates line numbers 100, 150, 200, and so on.

```
AUTO
```

Generates line numbers 10, 20, 30, 40, and so on.

BEEP Statement

Purpose:

To sound the speaker at 800 Hz (800 cycles per second) for one-quarter of a second.

Syntax:

BEEP

Comments:

BEEP, CTRL-G, and PRINT CHR$(7) have the same effect.

Examples:

```
2340 IF X>20 THEN BEEP
```

If X is out of range, the computer beeps.

BLOAD Command

Purpose:

To load an image file anywhere in user memory.

Syntax:

BLOAD *filename*[,*offset*]

Comments:

filename is a valid string expression containing the device and filename.

offset is a valid numeric expression within the range of 0 to 65535. This is the offset into the segment, declared by the last DEF SEG statement, where loading is to start.

If offset is omitted, the offset specified at BSAVE is assumed; that is, the file is loaded into the same location it was saved from.

Note

> BLOAD does not perform an address range check. It is possible to BLOAD anywhere in memory. You must not BLOAD over the GW-BASIC stack space, a GW-BASIC program, or the GW-BASIC variable area.

While BLOAD and BSAVE are useful for loading and saving machine language programs, they are not restricted to them. The DEF SEG statement lets you specify any segment as the source or target for BLOAD and BSAVE. For example, this allows the video screen buffer to be read from or written to the diskette. BLOAD and BSAVE are useful in saving and displaying graphic images.

Examples:

```
10 DEF SEG=&HB800
20 BLOAD"PICTURE",0
```

(This example may not work in some screen modes.)

The DEF SEG statement in line 10 points the segment at the screen buffer.

The DEF SEG statement in line 10 and the offset of 0 in line 20 guarantee that the correct address is used.

The BLOAD command in line 20 loads the file named *picture* into the screen buffer.

Note

The BSAVE example in the next section illustrates how the file named *picture* is saved.

BSAVE Command

Purpose:

To save portions of user memory on the specified device.

Syntax:

BSAVE *filename,offset,length*

Comments:

filename is a valid string expression containing the filename.

offset is a valid numeric expression within the range of 0 to 65535. This is the offset into the segment, declared by the last DEF SEG statement, where saving is to start.

length is a valid numeric expression within the range of 0 to 65535, specifying the length of the memory image to be saved.

If *filename* is less than one character, a "Bad File Number" error is issued and the load is aborted.

Execute a DEF SEG statement before the BSAVE. The last known DEF SEG address is always used for the save.

The DEF SEG statement must be used to set up the segment address to the start of the screen buffer. An offset of 0 and a length of 16384 specify that the entire 16K screen buffer is to be saved.

Examples:

```
10 DEF SEG=&HB800
20 BSAVE"PICTURE",0,16384
```

The DEF SEG statement in line 10 points the segment at the screen buffer.

The BSAVE command in line 20 saves the screen buffer in the file named *picture*.

CALL Statement

Purpose:

To call an assembly (or machine) language subroutine.

Syntax:

CALL *numvar*[*(variables)*]

Comments:

numvar is the starting point in memory of the subroutine being called as an offset into the current segment.

variables are the variables or constants, separated by commas and enclosed in parentheses, that are to be passed to the routine.

The CALL statement is recommended for interfacing assembly language programs with GW-BASIC. Although the USR function may also be used, CALL is compatible with more languages, produces a more readable source code, and can pass multiple arguments.

Invocation of the CALL statement causes the following to occur:

- Each parameter location in the variable is pushed onto the stack. The parameter location is a 2-byte offset into GW-BASIC's data segment.

- The return address code segment (CS) and the offset are pushed onto the stack.

- Control is transferred to the user routine by the segment address given in the last DEF SEG statement and the offset given in the variable name.

- The user routine now has control. Parameters may be referenced by moving the stack pointer (SP) to the base pointer (BP) and adding a positive offset to BP.

- The called routine may destroy the contents of any registers.

- The called program must know how many parameters were passed. Parameters are referenced by adding a positive offset to BP, assuming the called routine moved the current stack pointer into BP (that is, MOV BP,SP).

75

- The called program must know the variable type for numeric parameters passed.

- The called routine must do a RET *n*, where *n* is the number of parameters in the variable times 2. This is necessary in order to adjust the stack to the point at the start of the calling sequence.

- Values are returned to GW-BASIC by including in the argument list the name of the variable that is to receive the result.

- If the argument is a string, the parameter offset points to three bytes called the *string descriptor*. Byte 0 of the string descriptor contains the length of the string (0 to 255). Bytes 1 and 2, respectively, are the lower- and upper-eight bits of the string starting address in the string space.

- If the argument is a string literal in the program, the string descriptor points to program text. Be careful not to alter or destroy a program this way. To avoid unpredictable results, add +"" to the string literal in the program, as in the following:

```
20 A$="BASIC"+""
```

This forces the string literal to be copied into the string space. Now the string may be modified without affecting the program.

Note

Strings may be altered by user routines, but their length must not be changed. GW-BASIC cannot correctly erase strings if their lengths are modified by external routines.

For more information on the CALL statement and USR function, see Appendix D.

Example 1:

```
100 DEF SEG=&H2000
110 ARK=0
120 CALL ARK(A,B$,C)
  .
  .
  .
```

Line 100 sets the segment to hex 2000. ARK is set to zero so that the call to ARK executes the subroutine at location 2000:0.

Example 2:

The following sequence of 8086 Assembly Language demonstrates access of the parameters passed and stored in variable C:

```
PUSH BP
MOV BP,SP              ; Gets current stack position in BP.
MOV BX,8[BP]           ; Gets address of B$ descriptor.
MOV CL,[BX]            ; Gets length of B$ in CL.
MOV DX,1[BX]           ; Gets address of B$ text in DX.
   .
   .
   .
MOV SI,10[BP]          ; Gets address of A in SI.
MOV DI,6[BP]           ; Gets pointer to C in DI.
MOVSW                  ; Stores variable A in C.
RET 6                  ; Restores stack and returns.
```

MOVSW copies only two bytes. This is sufficient if variables A and C are integer. Four bytes must be copied if they are single precision; eight bytes, if they are double precision.

Example 3:

```
100 DEF SEG=&H2000
110 ACC=&H7FA
120 CALL ACC(A,B$,C)
   .
   .
   .
```

Line 100 sets the segment to hex 2000. The value of variable ACC is added into the address as the low word after the DEF SEG value is shifted four bits to the left (this is a function of the microprocessor, not of GW-BASIC). Here, ACC is set to &H7FA, so that the call to ACC executes the subroutine at the location hex 2000:7FA (absolute address hex 207FA).

CDBL Function

Purpose:

To convert x to a double-precision number.

Syntax:

CDBL(x)

Comments:

x must be a numeric expression.

Example:

```
10 A=454.67
20 PRINT A;CDBL(A)
RUN
454.67   454.6700134277344
Ok
```

Prints a double-precision version of the single-precision value stored in the variable named *A*.

The last 11 numbers in the double-precision number have no meaning in this example, since *A* was previously defined to only two-decimal place accuracy.

Note

See the CINT and CSNG functions for converting numbers to integer and single-precision, respectively.

CHAIN Statement

Purpose:

To transfer control to the specified program and pass (chain) variables to it from the current program.

Syntax:

CHAIN[MERGE] *filename*[,[*line*][,[**ALL**][,**DELETE** *range*]]]

Comments:

MERGE overlays the current program with the called program.

Note

> The called program must be an ASCII file (previously saved with the **a** option) if it is to be merged (see the MERGE command).

---

filename is the name of the program that is called to be chained to. The .BAS extension is assumed unless another is specified.

line is a line number or an expression that corresponds to a line number in the called program. It is the starting point for execution of the called program. For example, the following begins execution of PROG1 at line 1000:

```
10 CHAIN "PROG1",1000
```

If *line* is omitted, execution begins at the first line.

line is not affected by a RENUM command. However, the line numbers in the specified range are affected by a RENUM command.

ALL specifies that every variable in the current program is chained to the called program. For example:

```
20 CHAIN "PROG1",1000,ALL
```

If the ALL option is omitted, the current program must contain a
COMMON statement to list the variables that are passed.

CHAIN executes a RESTORE before it runs the program that it is to be
chained to. The READ statement then gets the first item in the DATA
statement. Reading will not resume where it left off in the program that
is being chained.

After an overlay is executed and used for a specific purpose, it is usually
desirable to delete it so that a new overlay may be brought in. To do this,
use the DELETE command.

The CHAIN statement with the MERGE command leaves the files open and
preserves the current option base setting.

If the MERGE command is omitted, the OPTION BASE setting is preserved, and CHAIN preserves no variable types or user-defined functions
for use by the chained program. That is, any DEFINT, DEFSNG, DEFDBL,
DEFSTR, or DEF FN statement containing shared variables must be re-
stated in the chained program.

When using the MERGE command, place user-defined functions before any
CHAIN MERGE statements in the program. Otherwise, they will be undefined after the merge is complete.

CHDIR Command

Purpose:

To change from one working directory to another.

Syntax:

CHDIR *pathname*

Comments:

pathname is a string expression of up to 63 characters.

To make *sales* the working directory on Drive A: and *inventory* the working directory on Drive B: (assume A: is the default drive), type the following commands:

```
CHDIR "SALES"
CHDIR "B:INVENTORY"
```

CHR$ Function

Purpose:

To convert an ASCII code to its equivalent character.

Syntax:

CHR$(*n*)

Comments:

n is a value from 0 to 255.

CHR$ is commonly used to send a special character to the terminal or printer. For example, you could send CHR$(7) to sound a beep through the speaker as a preface to an error message, or you could send a form feed, CHR$(12), to the printer.

See the ASC function for ASCII-to-numeric conversion.

ASCII codes are listed in Appendix C.

Examples:

```
PRINT CHR$(66);
B
Ok
```

This prints the ASCII character code 66, which is the uppercase letter *B*.

```
PRINT CHR$(13);
```

This command prints a carriage return.

CINT Function

Purpose:

To round numbers with fractional portions to the next whole number or integer.

Syntax:

CINT(*x*)

Comments:

If x is not within the range of -32768 to 32767, an "Overflow" error occurs.

See the FIX and INT functions, both of which return integers.

Examples:

```
PRINT CINT(45.67)
46
Ok
```

45.67 is rounded up to 46.

Note

See the CDBL and CSNG functions for converting numbers to the double-precision and single-precision data types, respectively.

CIRCLE Statement

Purpose:

To draw a circle, ellipse, and angles on the screen during use of the Graphics mode.

Syntax:

CIRCLE(*xcenter,ycenter*),*radius*[,[*color*][,[*start*],[*end*][,*aspect*]]]

Comments:

xcenter and *ycenter* are the x- and y- coordinates of the center of the ellipse, and *radius* is the radius (measured along the major axis) of the ellipse. The quantities *xcenter* and *ycenter* can be expressions. The center attributes can use either absolute or relative coordinates.

color specifies the color of the ellipse. Its value depends on the current screen mode.

See the COLOR and SCREEN statements for more information on using colors in the different screen modes.

In the high-resolution mode, 0 indicates black and 1 indicates white. The default for the high-resolution mode is 1.

The *start* and *end* angle parameters are radian arguments between $-2*\pi$ and $2*\pi$ that specify where the drawing of the ellipse is to begin and end. If *start* or *end* is negative, the ellipse is connected to the center point with a line, and the angles are treated as if they are positive (note that this is different from adding $2*\pi$).

aspect describes the ratio of the x radius to the y radius (x:y). The default aspect ratio depends on the screen mode, but gives a visual circle in either graphics mode, assuming a standard monitor screen aspect ratio of 4:3.

If the aspect ratio is less than 1, then the radius is given in x-pixels. If it is greater than 1, the radius is given in y-pixels.

In many cases, an aspect ratio of 1 gives better ellipses in the medium-resolution mode. This also causes the ellipse to be drawn faster. The start angle may be less than the end angle.

Example 1:

```
10 SCREEN1: CIRCLE(100,100), 50
```

Draws a circle of radius 50, centered at graphics points 100x and 100y.

Example 2:

```
1  ' This will draw 17 ellipses
10 CLS
20 SCREEN 1
30 FOR R=160 TO 0 STEP-10
40 CIRCLE (160,100),R,,,,5/18
50 NEXT
```

Example 3:

```
10 'This will draw 5 spheres
20 GOTO 160
50 IF VERT GOTO 100
60 CIRCLE (X,Y),R,C,,,.07
70 FOR I = 1 TO 5
80 CIRCLE (X,Y),R,C,,,I*.2:NEXT I
90 IF VERT THEN RETURN
100 CIRCLE (X,Y),R,C,,,1.3
110 CIRCLE (X,Y),R,C,,,1.9
120 CIRCLE (X,Y),R,C,,,3.6
130 CIRCLE (X,Y),R,C,,,9.8
140 IF VERT GOTO 60
150 RETURN
160 CLS:SCREEN 1:COLOR 0,1:KEY OFF:VERT=0
170 X=160:Y=100:C=1:R=50:GOSUB 50
180 X=30:Y=30:C=2:R=30:GOSUB 50
190 X=30:Y=169:GOSUB 50
200 X=289:Y=30:GOSUB 50
210 X=289:Y=169:GOSUB 50
220 LINE (30,30)-(289,169),1
230 LINE (30,169)-(289,30),1
240 LINE (30,169)-(289,30),1,B
250 Z$=INKEY$: IF Z$="" THEN 250
RUN
```

CLEAR Command

Purpose:

To set all numeric variables to zero, all string variables to null, and to close all open files. Options set the end of memory and reserve the amount of string and stack space available for use by GW-BASIC.

Syntax:

CLEAR[,[*expression1***][,***expression2***]]**

Comments:

expression1 is a memory location that, if specified, sets the maximum number of bytes available for use by GW-BASIC.

expression2 sets aside stack space for GW-BASIC. The default is the previous stack space size. When GW-BASIC is first executed, the stack space is set to 512 bytes, or one-eighth of the available memory, whichever is smaller.

GW-BASIC allocates string space dynamically. An "Out of String Space" error occurs only if there is no free memory left for GW-BASIC to use.

The CLEAR command:

- Closes all files
- Clears all COMMON and user variables
- Resets the stack and string space
- Releases all disk buffers
- Turns off any sound
- Resets sound to music foreground
- Resets PEN to *off*
- Resets STRIG to *off*
- Disables ON ERROR trapping

Examples:

CLEAR

Zeroes variables and nulls all strings.

CLEAR 32768

Zeroes variables, nulls strings, protects memory above 32768, does not change the stack space.

CLEAR , ,2000

Zeroes variables, nulls strings, allocates 2000 bytes for stack space, and uses all available memory in the segment.

CLEAR ,32768,2000

Zeroes variables, nulls strings, protects memory above 32768, and allocates 2000 bytes for stack space.

CLOSE Statement

Purpose:

To terminate input/output to a disk file or a device.

Syntax:

CLOSE [[#]*filenumber*[,[#]*filenumber*]...]

Comments:

filenumber is the number under which the file was opened.

The association between a particular file or device and file number terminates upon execution of a CLOSE statement. The file or device can then be reopened using the same or a different file number.

A CLOSE statement with no file number specified closes all open files and devices.

A CLOSE statement sent to a file or device opened for sequential output writes the final buffer of output to that file or device.

The END, NEW, RESET, SYSTEM, or RUN and LOAD (without **r** option) statements always close all files or devices automatically. STOP does not close files.

Examples:

```
250 CLOSE
```

This closes all open devices and files.

```
300 CLOSE 1,#2,#3
```

Closes all files and devices associated with file numbers 1, 2, and 3.

CLS Statement

Purpose:

To clear the screen.

Syntax:

CLS [*n*]

Comments:

n is one of the following values:

Value of *n*	Effect
0	Clears the screen of all text and graphics
1	Clears only the graphics viewport
2	Clears only the text window

If the graphics viewport is active, CLS without argument clears only the viewport. If the graphics viewport is inactive, CLS clears the text window.

If the screen is in alpha mode, the active page is cleared to the currently selected background color (see the SCREEN and COLOR statements).

If the screen is in graphics mode, the entire screen buffer is cleared to background color.

The screen may also be cleared by pressing CTRL-HOME, or by changing the screen mode with the SCREEN or WIDTH statements.

CLS returns the cursor to the upper-left corner of the screen, and sets the last point referenced to the center of the screen.

If the VIEW statement has been used, CLS clears only the last viewport specified.

Examples:

```
1 CLS
```

This clears the screen.

COLOR Statement

Purpose:

To select display colors

Syntax:

COLOR [*foreground*][,[*background*][,*border*]]
COLOR [*background*][,[*palette*]]
COLOR [*foreground*][,[*background*]]

Comments:

In general, COLOR allows you to select the foreground and background colors for the display. In SCREEN 0 a border color can also be selected. In SCREEN 1 no foreground color can be selected, but one of two four-color palettes can be selected for use with graphics statements. The different syntaxes and effects that apply to the various screen modes are described below:

Mode	Effect
SCREEN 0	Modifies the current default text foreground and background colors, and the screen border. The *foreground* color must be an integer expression in the range $0-31$. It is used to determine the "foreground" color in text mode, which is the default color of text. Sixteen colors can be selected with the integers $0-15$. A blinking version of each color can be selected by adding 16 to the color number; for example, a blinking color 7 is equal to $7 + 16$, or 23. Thus, the legal integer range for *foreground* is $0-31$.
	The *background* color must be an integer expression in the range $0-7$, and is the color of the background for each text character. Blinking colors are not permitted.
	The *border* color is an integer expression in the range $0-15$, and is the color used when drawing the screen border. Blinking colors are not permitted.

If no arguments are provided to COLOR, then the default color for *background* and *border* is black (color 0), and for *foreground*, is as described in the SCREEN statement reference pages.

SCREEN 1   In mode 1, the COLOR statement has a unique syntax that includes a *palette* argument, which is an odd or even integer expression. This argument determines the set of display colors to use when displaying particular color numbers.

For hardware configurations that do not have an IBM® Enhanced Graphics Adapter (EGA), the default color settings for the *palette* parameter are equivalent to the following:

```
COLOR ,0      'Same as the next three PALETTE
              'statements
              '1 = green, 2 = red, 3 = yellow

COLOR ,1      'Same as the next three PALETTE
              'statements
              '1 = cyan, 2 = magenta, 3 = hi.
              'intens. white
```

With the EGA, the default color settings for the *palette* parameter are equivalent to the following:

```
COLOR ,0      'Same as the next three PALETTE
              'statements
PALETTE 1,2   'Attribute 1 = color 3 (green)
PALETTE 2,4   'Attribute 2 = color 5 (red)
PALETTE 3,6   'Attribute 3 = color 6 (brown)

COLOR ,1      'Same as the next three PALETTE
              'statements
PALETTE 1,3   'Attribute 1 = color 3 (cyan)
PALETTE 2,5   'Attribute 2 = color 5 (magenta)
PALETTE 3,7   'Attribute 3 = color 15 (white)
```

Note that a COLOR statement will override previous PALETTE statements.

SCREEN 2   No effect. An "Illegal function call" error occurs if COLOR is used in this mode.

SCREEN 7—
SCREEN 10 In these modes, no *border* color can be specified. The graphics background is given by the *background* color number, which must be in the valid range of color numbers appropriate to the screen mode. See the SCREEN statement reference pages for more details. The *foreground* color argument is the default line drawing color.

Arguments outside valid numeric ranges result in "Illegal function call" errors.

The foreground color may be the same as the background color, making displayed characters invisible. The default background color is black, or color number 0, for all display hardware configurations and all screen modes.

With the Enhanced Graphics Adapter (EGA) installed, the PALETTE statement gives you flexibility in assigning different display colors to the actual color-number ranges for the *foreground*, *background*, and *border* colors discussed above. See the PALETTE statement reference pages for more details.

For more information, see CIRCLE, DRAW, LINE, PAINT, PALETTE, PRESET, PSET, SCREEN

Examples:

The following series of examples show COLOR statements and their effects in the various screen modes:

```
SCREEN  0
COLOR   1, 2, 3   'foreground=1, background=2, border=3

SCREEN  1
COLOR   1,0       'foreground=1, even palette number
COLOR   2,1       'foreground=2, odd palette number

SCREEN  7
COLOR   3,5       'foreground=3, background=5

SCREEN  8
COLOR   6,7       'foreground=6, background=7

SCREEN  9
COLOR   1,2       'foreground=1, background=2
```

COM(n) Statement

Purpose:

To enable or disable trapping of communications activity to the specified communications adapter.

Syntax:

COM(*n*) ON
COM(*n*) OFF
COM(*n*) STOP

Comments:

n is the number of the communications adapter 1 or 2.

Execute a COM(*n*) ON statement before an ON COM(*n*) statement to allow trapping. After COM(*n*) ON, if a nonzero number is specified in the ON COM(*n*) statement, BASIC checks every new statement to see if any characters have come in the communications adapter.

With COM(*n*) OFF, no trapping takes place, and all communications activity will be lost.

With COM(*n*) STOP, no trapping takes place. However, any communication that takes place will be remembered so that immediate trapping will occur when COM(*n*) ON is executed.

COMMON Statement

Purpose:

To pass variables to a chained program.

Syntax:

COMMON *variables*

Comments:

variables are one or more variables, separated by commas, that you want to pass to the chained program.

The COMMON statement is used in conjunction with the CHAIN statement.

COMMON statements may appear anywhere in a program, although it is recommended that they appear at the beginning.

Any number of COMMON statements may appear in a program, but the same variable cannot appear in more than one COMMON statement. To pass all variables using the CHAIN statement, use the ALL option, and omit the COMMON statement.

Place parentheses after the variable name to indicate array variables.

Examples:

```
100 COMMON A, B, C, D( ),G$
110 CHAIN "A:PROG3"
```

This example chains to program PROG3 on disk drive A:, and passes the array D along with the variables A, B, C, and string G$.

CONT Command

Purpose:

To continue program execution after a break.

Syntax:

CONT

Comments:

Resumes program execution after CTRL-BREAK, STOP, or END halts a program. Execution continues at the point where the break happened. If the break took place during an INPUT statement, execution continues after reprinting the prompt.

CONT is useful in debugging, in that it lets you set break points with the STOP statement, modify variables using direct statements, continue program execution, or use GOTO to resume execution at a particular line number.

If a program line is modified, CONT will be invalid.

COS Function

Purpose:

To return the cosine of the range of x.

Syntax:

COS(x)

Comments:

x must be the radians. COS is the trigonometric cosine function. To convert from degrees to radians, multiply by $\pi/180$.

COS(x) is calculated in single-precision unless the **/d** switch is used when GW-BASIC is executed.

Example 1:

```
10 X=2*COS(.4)
20 PRINT X
RUN
 1.842122
Ok
```

Example 2:

```
10 PI=3.141593
20 PRINT COS(PI)
30 DEGREES=180
40 RADIANS=DEGREES*PI/180
50 PRINT COS(RADIANS)
RUN
-1
-1
OK
```

CSNG Function

Purpose:

To convert x to a single-precision number.

Syntax:

CSNG(*x*)

Comments:

x must be a numeric expression (see the CINT and CDBL functions).

Examples:

```
10 A#=975.3421222#
20 PRINT A#; CSNG(A#)
RUN
  975.3421222    975.3421
Ok
```

CSRLIN Variable

Purpose:

To return the current line (row) position of the cursor.

Syntax:

y = CSRLIN

Comments:

y is a numeric variable receiving the value returned. The value returned is within the range of 1 to 25.

The CSRLIN Variable returns the vertical coordinate of the cursor on the active page (see the SCREEN statement).

x = POS(0) returns the column location of the cursor. The value returned is within the range of 1 to 40, or 1 to 80, depending on the current screen width (see the POS function).

Examples:

```
10  Y=CSRLIN
20  X=POS(0)
30  LOCATE 24,1
40  PRINT "HELLO"
50  LOCATE Y,X
RUN
HELLO
Ok
```

The CSRLIN Variable in line 10 records the current line.

The POS function in line 20 records the current column.

In line 40, the PRINT statement displays the comment "HELLO" on the 24th line of the screen.

The LOCATE statement in line 50 restores the position of the cursor to the original line and column.

CVI, CVS, CVD Functions

Purpose:

To convert string values to numeric values.

Syntax:

CVI(*2-byte string*)
CVS(*4-byte string*)
CVD(*8-byte string*)

Comments:

Numeric values read in from a random-access disk file must be converted from strings back into numbers if they are to be arithmetically manipulated.

CVI converts a 2-byte string to an integer. MKI$ is its complement.

CVS converts a 4-byte string to a single-precision number. MKS$ is its complement.

CVD converts an 8-byte string to a double-precision number. MKD$ is its complement.

(See MKI$, MKS$, and MKD$.)

Examples:

```
.
.
.
70 FIELD #1,4 AS N$, 12 AS B$...
80 GET #1
90 Y=CVS(N$)
.
.
.
```

Line 80 reads a field from file #1 (the field read is defined in line 70), and converts the first four bytes (N$) into a single-precision number assigned to the variable Y.

Since a single-precision number can contain as many as seven ASCII characters (seven bytes), when writing a file using MKS$ conversion, and reading with the CVS conversion, as many as three bytes per number recorded are saved on the storage medium. Even more may be saved if double-precision numbers are required. MKD$ and CVD conversions would be used in this case.

DATA Statement

Purpose:

To store the numeric and string constants that are accessed by the program READ statement(s).

Syntax:

DATA *constants*

Comments:

constants are numeric constants in any format (fixed point, floating-point, or integer), separated by commas. No expressions are allowed in the list.

String constants in DATA statements must be surrounded by double quotation marks only if they contain commas, colons, or significant leading or trailing spaces. Otherwise, quotation marks are not needed.

DATA statements are not executable and may be placed anywhere in the program. A DATA statement can contain as many constants as will fit on a line (separated by commas), and any number of DATA statements can be used in a program.

READ statements access the DATA statements in order (by line number). The data contained therein may be thought of as one continuous list of items, regardless of how many items are on a line or where the lines are placed in the program. The variable type (numeric or string) given in the READ statement must agree with the corresponding constant in the DATA statement, or a "Type Mismatch" error occurs.

DATA statements may be reread from the beginning by use of the RESTORE statement.

For further information and examples, see the RESTORE statement and the READ statement.

Example 1:

.
.
.
```
80 FOR I=1 TO 10
90 READ A(I)
100 NEXT I
110 DATA 3.08,5.19,3.12,3.98,4.24
120 DATA 5.08,5.55,4.00,3.16,3.37
```
.
.
.

This program segment reads the values from the DATA statements into array A. After execution, the value of A(1) is 3.08, and so on. The DATA statements (lines 110–120) may be placed anywhere in the program; they may even be placed ahead of the READ statement.

Example 2:

```
5 PRINT
10 PRINT "CITY","STATE","ZIP"
20 READ C$,S$,Z
30 DATA "DENVER,","COLORADO",80211
40 PRINT C$,S$,Z
RUN

CITY            STATE           ZIP
DENVER,         COLORADO           80211
Ok
```

This program reads string and numeric data from the DATA statement in line 30.

DATE$ Statement and Variable

Purpose:

To set or retrieve the current date.

Syntax:

As a statement:

DATE$ = v$

As a variable:

v$ = DATE$

Comments:

v$ is a valid string literal or variable.

v$ can be any of the following formats when assigning the date:

mm-dd-yy
mm/dd/yy
mm-dd-yyyy
mm/dd/yyyy

If v$ is not a valid string, a "Type Mismatch" error results. Previous values are retained.

If any of the values are out of range or missing, an "Illegal Function Call" error is issued. Any previous date is retained.

The current date (as assigned when the operating system was initialized) is fetched and assigned to the string variable if DATE$ is the expression in a LET or PRINT statement.

The current date is stored if DATE$ is the target of a string assignment.

With v$ = DATE$, DATE$ returns a 10-character string in the form mm-dd-yyyy. mm is the month (01 to 12), dd is the day (01 to 31), and yyyy is the year (1980 to 2099).

Examples:

```
v$=DATE$
Ok
PRINT V$
01-01-1985
Ok
```

DEF FN Statement

Purpose:

To define and name a function written by the user.

Syntax:

DEF FNname[arguments] expression

Comments:

name must be a legal variable name. This name, preceded by FN, becomes the name of the function.

arguments consists of those variable names in the function definition that are to be replaced when the function is called. The items in the list are separated by commas.

expression is an expression that performs the operation of the function. It is limited to one statement

In the DEF FN statement, arguments serve only to define the function; they do not affect program variables that have the same name. A variable name used in a function definition may or may not appear in the argument. If it does, the value of the parameter is supplied when the function is called. Otherwise, the current value of the variable is used.

The variables in the argument represent, on a one-to-one basis, the argument variables or values that are to be given in the function call.

User-defined functions may be numeric or string. If a type is specified in the function name, the value of the expression is forced to that type before it is returned to the calling statement. If a type is specified in the function name and the argument type does not match, a "Type Mismatch" error occurs.

A user-defined function may be defined more than once in a program by repeating the DEF FN statement.

A DEF FN statement must be executed before the function it defines may be called. If a function is called before it has been defined, an "Undefined User Function" error occurs.

DEF FN is illegal in the direct mode.

Recursive functions are not supported in the DEF FN statement.

Examples:

```
       .
       .
       .
400  R=1:S=2
410  DEF FNAB(X,Y)=X^3/Y^2
420  T=FNAB(R,S)
       .
       .
       .
```

Line 410 defines the user-defined function FNAB. The function is called in line 420. When executed, the variable T will contain the value R^3 divided by S^2, or .25.

DEFINT/SNG/DBL/STR Statements

Purpose:

To declare variable types as integer, single-precision, double-precision, or string.

Syntax:

DEF*type letters*

Comments:

type is INT (integer), SNG (single-precision number), DBL (double-precision number), or STR (string of 0–255 characters).

letters are letters (separated by commas) or range of letters of the alphabet.

A DEF*type* statement declares that variable names beginning with the letter(s) specify that type of variable. However, a type declaration character (%,!,#,$) always takes precedence over a DEF*type* statement in the typing of a variable.

If no type declaration statements are encountered, BASIC assumes all variables are single-precision. Single-precision is the default value.

Examples:

```
10 DEFDBL L-P
```

All variables beginning with the letters L, M, N, O, or P will be double-precision variables.

```
10 DEFSTR A
20 A="120#"
```

All variables beginning with the letter A will be string variables. The $ declaration is unnecessary in this example.

```
10 DEFINT I-N,W-Z
20 W$="120#"
```

All variables beginning with the letters I, J, K, L, M, N, W, X, Y, or Z will be integer variables. W$ in Line 20 establishes a string variable beginning with the letter W. However, the variable W will remain an integer elsewhere in the program.

DEF SEG Statement

Purpose:

To assign the current segment address to be referenced by a subsequent BLOAD, BSAVE, CALL, PEEK, POKE, or USR.

Syntax:

DEF SEG [*address*]

Comments:

address is a numeric expression within the range of 0 to 65535.

The address specified is saved for use as the segment required by BLOAD, BSAVE, PEEK, POKE, and CALL statements.

Entry of any value outside the address range (0–65535) results in an "Illegal Function Call" error, and the previous value is retained.

If the address option is omitted, the segment to be used is set to GW-BASIC's data segment (DS). This is the initial default value.

If you specify the address option, base it on a 16-byte boundary.

Segment addresses are shifted 4 bits to the left; so to get the segment address, divide the memory location by 16.

For BLOAD, BSAVE, PEEK, POKE, or CALL statements, the value is shifted left four bits (this is done by the microprocessor, not by GW-BASIC) to form the code segment address for the subsequent call instruction (see the BLOAD, BSAVE, CALL, PEEK, and POKE statements).

GW-BASIC does not perform additional checking to assure that the resultant segment address is valid.

Examples:

```
10 DEF SEG=&HB800
```

Sets segment to screen buffer.

```
20 DEF SEG
```

Restores segment to BASIC DS.

Note

DEF and SEG must be separated by a space. Otherwise, GW-BASIC will interpret the statement DEFSEG = 100 to mean, "assign the value 100 to the variable DEFSEG."

DEF USR Statement

Purpose:

To specify the starting address of an assembly language subroutine to be called from memory by the USR function.

Syntax:

DEF USR[*n*] = *integer*

Comments:

n may be any digit from 0 to 9. The digit corresponds to the USR routine address being specified. If *n* is omitted, DEF USR0 is assumed.

integer is the offset address of the USR routine. If more than 10 USR routines are required, DEF USR[*n*] may appear in the program as many times as necessary to redefine the USR[*n*] starting address.

Add the current segment value to the integer to get the starting address of the user routine.

When an Assembly Language Subroutine is called, the GW-BASIC program execution is paused, and control is transferred to the Assembly Language program. When that program is executed, control is returned to the GW-BASIC program at the point of interruption.

Examples:

```
.
.
.
190 DEF SEG=0
200 DEF USR0=24000
210 X=USR0(Y^2/2.82)
.
.
.
```

Lines 190 and 200 set the absolute address.

Line 210 calls the USR routine located at that address, and passes the integer value of the expression contained within the parentheses to the user program (see USR).

Note

This statement is given here primarily to provide compatibility with other GW-BASIC implementations. The more versatile CALL statement should be used if this downward compatibility is unimportant.

DELETE Command

Purpose:

To delete program lines or line ranges.

Syntax:

DELETE [*line number1*][*-line number2*]
DELETE *line number1-*

Comments:

line number1 is the first line to be deleted.

line number2 is the last line to be deleted.

GW-BASIC always returns to command level after a DELETE command is executed. Unless at least one line number is given, an "Illegal Function Call" error occurs.

The period (.) may be used to substitute for either line number to indicate the current line.

Examples:

```
DELETE 40
```

Deletes line 40.

```
DELETE 40-100
```

Deletes lines 40 through 100, inclusively.

```
DELETE -40
```

Deletes all lines up to and including line 40.

```
DELETE 40-
```

Deletes all lines from line 40 to the end of the program.

DIM Statement

Purpose:

To specify the maximum values for array variable subscripts and allocate storage accordingly.

Syntax:

DIM *variable(subscripts)*[,*variable(subscripts)*]...

Comments:

If an array variable name is used without a DIM statement, the maximum value of its subscript(s) is assumed to be 10. If a subscript greater than the maximum specified is used, a "Subscript out of range" error occurs.

The maximum number of dimensions for an array is 255.

The minimum value for a subscript is always 0, unless otherwise specified with the OPTION BASE statement.

An array, once dimensioned, cannot be redimensioned within the program without first executing a CLEAR or ERASE statement.

The DIM statement sets all the elements of the specified arrays to an initial value of zero.

Examples:

```
10 DIM A(20)
20 FOR I=0 TO 20
30 READ A(I)
40 NEXT I
```

This example reads 21 DATA statements elsewhere in the program and assigns their values to A(0) through A(20), sequentially and inclusively. If the A array is single-precision (default accuracy) then line 10 will allocate 84 bytes of memory to this array (4 bytes times 21 elements).

DRAW Statement

Purpose:

To draw a figure.

Syntax:

DRAW *string expression*

Comments:

The DRAW statement combines most of the capabilities of the other graphics statements into an object definition language called the Graphics Macro Language (GML). A GML command is a single character within a string, optionally followed by one or more arguments.

The DRAW statement is valid only in graphics mode.

Movement Commands

Each of the following movement commands begins movement from the current graphics position. This is usually the coordinate of the last graphics point plotted with another GML command, LINE, or PSET. The current position defaults to the center of the screen (160,100 in medium resolution; 320,100 in high resolution) when a program is run. Movement commands move for a distance of scale factor *n, where the default for n is 1; thus, they move one point if n is omitted and the default scale factor is used.

Command	Moves
Un	up
Dn	down
Ln	left
Rn	right
En	diagonally up and right
Fn	diagonally down and right

G*n*   diagonally down and left

H*n*   diagonally up and left

This command moves as specified by the following argument:

M*x,y*   Move absolute or relative. If *x* is preceded by a +
                        or −, *x* and *y* are added to the current graphics
                        position, and connected to the current position by a
                        line. Otherwise, a line is drawn to point *x,y* from
                        the current position.

The following prefix commands may precede any of the above movement
commands:

B   Move, but plot no points.

N   Move, but return to original position when done.

The following commands are also available:

A*n*   Set angle *n*. *n* may range from 0 to 3, where 0 is 0°,
                        1 is 90°, 2 is 180°, and 3 is 270°. Figures rotated 90°
                        or 270° are scaled so that they will appear the same
                        size as with 0° or 180° on a monitor screen with the
                        standard aspect ratio of 4:3.

TA*n*   Turn angle *n*. *n* can be any value from negative 360
                        to positive 360. If the value specified by *n* is posi-
                        tive, it turns the angle counterclockwise. If the
                        value specified by *n* is negative, it turns clockwise.

C*n*   Set color *n*. See the COLOR, PALETTE, and
                        SCREEN statements for discussions of valid colors,
                        numbers, and attributes.

S*n*   Set scale factor. *n* may range from 1 to 255. *n* is
                        divided by 4 to derive the scale factor. The scale
                        factor is multiplied by the distances given with U,
                        D, L, R, E, F, G, H, or relative M commands to get
                        the actual distance traveled. The default for S is 4.

x*string*; *variable*   Execute substring. This command executes a second
                        substring from a string, much like GOSUB. One
                        string executes another, which executes a third,
                        and so on.

                        string is a variable assigned to a string of move-
                        ment commands.

117

Ppaint, boundary   Specifies the colors for a graphics figure and creates a filled-in figure.

paint specifies what color you want the figure filled in with.

boundary specifies the border color (outline).

See the COLOR, PALETTE, and SCREEN statements for discussions of valid colors, numbers, and attributes.

You must specify values for both paint and boundary when used.

This command (Ppaint,boundary) does not paint color tiling.

Numeric Arguments:

Numeric arguments can be constants like "123" or "=variable;", where variable is the name of a variable.

When you use the second syntax, "=variable;", the semicolon must be used. Otherwise, the semicolon is optional between commands.

You can also specify variables using VARPTR$(variable).

Example 1:

To draw a box in medium resolution:

```
10 SCREEN 1
20 A=20
30 DRAW "U=A;R=A;D=A;L=A;"
RUN
```

Example 2:

The aspect ratio to draw a square on a standard screen is 4:3, as shown below:

To draw a 96-pixel-wide square on a 640×200 pixel screen (SCREEN 2), do the following calculations:

Horizontal value = 96
Vertical value = 96*(200/640)*(4/3)

or

Vertical value = 40
Horizontal value = 40*(640/200)*(3/4)

The horizontal values equals 4/3 of the vertical values.

Example 3:

To draw a triangle in medium resolution:

```
10 CLS
20 SCREEN 1
30 PSET (60,125)
40 DRAW "E100; F100; L199"
RUN
```

EDIT Command

Purpose:

To display a specified line, and to position the cursor under the first digit of the line number, so that the line may be edited.

Syntax:

EDIT *line number*
EDIT .

Comments:

line number is the number of a line existing in the program.

A period (.) refers to the current line. The following command enters EDIT at the current line:

```
EDIT  .
```

When a line is entered, it becomes the current line.

The current line is always the last line referenced by an EDIT statement, LIST command, or error message.

If *line number* refers to a line that does not exist in the program, an "Undefined Line Number" error occurs.

Examples:

```
EDIT 150
```

Displays program line number 150 for editing.

END Statement

Purpose:

To terminate program execution, close all files, and return to command level.

Syntax:

END

Comments:

END statements may be placed anywhere in the program to terminate execution.

Unlike the STOP statement, END does not cause a "Break in line *xxxx*" message to be printed.

An END statement at the end of a program is optional. GW-BASIC always returns to command level after an END is executed.

END closes all files.

Examples:

```
520 IF K>1000 THEN END ELSE GOTO 20
```

Ends the program and returns to command level whenever the value of K exceeds 1000.

ENVIRON Statement

Purpose:

To allow the user to modify parameters in GW-BASIC's environment string table. This may be to change the path parameter for a child process, (see ENVIRON$, SHELL, and the MS-DOS utilities PATH command), or to pass parameters to a child by inventing a new environment parameter.

Syntax:

ENVIRON *string*

Comments:

string is a valid string expression containing the new environment string parameter.

string must be of the following form

parmid = text

where *parmid* is the name of the parameter, such as PATH.

parmid must be separated from text by an equal sign or a blank. ENVIRON takes everything to the left of the first blank or equal sign as the *parmid*; everything following is taken as text.

text is the new parameter text. If *text* is a null string, or consists only of a single semicolon, then the parameter (including *parmid =*) is removed from the environment string table, and the table is compressed. *text* must not contain any embedded blanks.

If *parmid* does not exist, then *string* is added at the end of the environment string table.

If *parmid* does exist, it is deleted, the environment string table is compressed, and the new string is added at the end.

Examples:

Assuming the environment string table is empty, the following statement will create a default path to the root directory on Disk A:

```
ENVIRON "PATH=A:\"
```

If your work subdirectory were *john*, you would be able to get DEBUG from the root.

A new parameter may be added:

```
ENVIRON "COMSPEC=A:\COMMAND.COM"
```

The environment string table now contains

```
PATH=A:\;COMSPEC=A:\COMMAND.COM
```

The path may be changed to a new value:

```
ENVIRON "PATH=A:\SALES;A:\ACCOUNTING"
```

The path parameter may be appended by using the ENVIRON$ function with the ENVIRON statement:

```
ENVIRON "PATH="+ENVIRON$("PATH")+";B:\SAMPLES"
```

Finally, delete the parameter COMSPEC:

```
ENVIRON "COMSPEC=;"
```

The environment string table now contains

```
PATH=A:\SALES;A:\ACCOUNTING;B:\SAMPLES
```

ENVIRON$ Function

Purpose:

To allow the user to retrieve the specified environment string from the environment table.

Syntax:

v\$ = ENVIRON\$(*parmid***)**
v\$ = ENVIRON\$(*nthparm***)**

Comments:

parmid is a valid string expression containing the parameter to search for.

nthparm is an integer expression in the range of 1 to 255.

If a string argument is used, ENVIRON\$ returns a string containing the text following *parmid* = from the environment string table.

If *parmid* is not found, then a null string is returned.

If a numeric argument is used, ENVIRON\$ returns a string containing the *nth* parameter from the environment string table.

If there is no *nth* parameter, then a null string is returned.

The ENVIRON\$ function distinguishes between upper- and lowercase.

Examples:

The following lines:

```
ENVIRON "PATH=A:\SALES;A:\ACOUNTING;B:\MKT:" 'Create entry
PRINT ENVIRON$("PATH")  'Print entry
```

will print the following string:

```
A:\SALES;A:\ACCOUNTING;B:\MKT
```

The following line will print the first string in the environment:

```
PRINT ENVIRON$(1)
```

The following program saves the environment string table in an array so that it can be modified for a child process. After the child process completes, the environment is restored.

```
10    DIM ENVTBL$(10) "
20    NPARMS= 1
30    WHILE LEN(ENVIRON$(NPARMS)) #0
40    ENVTBL$ (NPARMS)= ENVIRON$(NPARMS)
50    NPARMS= NPARMS + 1
60    WEND
70    NPARMS= NPARMS-1
72    WHILE LEN(ENVIRON$(1))#0
73    A$=MID$(ENVIRON$(1),1,INSTR (ENVIRON$(1),"="))
74    ENVIRON A$+";"
75    WEND
90    ENVIRON "MYCHILDPARM1=SORT BY NAME"
100   ENVIRON "MYCHILDPARM2=LIST BY NAME"
          .
          .
          .
1000 SHELL "MYCHILD"'RUNS "MYCHILD.EXE"
1002 WHILE LEN(ENVIRON$(1))#0
1003 A$=MID$(ENVIRON$(1),1,INSTR(ENVIRON$ (1),"="))
1004 ENVIRON A$+";"
1005 WEND
1010 FOR I=1 TO NPARMS
1020 ENVIRON ENVTBL$(I)
1030 NEXT I
          .
          .
          .
```

The DIM statement in line 10 assumes no more than 10 parameters will be accessed.

In line 20, the initial number of parameters is established as 1.

In lines 30 through 70, a series of statements are used to adjust and correct the paramenter numbers.

Line 71 deletes the present environment.

Lines 72 through 80 create a new environment. Line 74 deletes the string.

Lines 80 through 100 store the new environment.

Lines 1000 through 1030 repeat the procedure by deleting the present environment and restore the parameters established in the first part of the program.

EOF Function

Purpose:

To return -1 (true) when the end of a sequential or a communications file has been reached, or to return 0 if end of file (EOF) has not been found.

Syntax:

$\mathbf{v} = \mathbf{EOF}(\textit{file number})$

Comments:

If a GET is done past the end of the file, EOF returns -1. This may be used to find the size of a file using a binary search or other algorithm. With communications files, a -1 indicates that the buffer is empty.

Use EOF to test for the end of the file while inputting to avoid "Input Past End" errors.

Examples:

```
10 OPEN "I",1,"DATA"
20 C=0
30 IF EOF(1) THEN 100
40 INPUT#1,M(C)
50 C=C+1:GOTO 30
100 END
RUN
```

The file named DATA is read into the M array until the end of the file is reached, then the program branches to line 100.

ERASE Statement

Purpose:

To eliminate arrays from a program.

Syntax:

ERASE *list of array variables*

Comments:

Arrays may be redimensioned after they are erased, or the memory space previously allocated to the array may be used for other purposes.

If an attempt is made to redimension an array without first erasing it, an error occurs.

Examples:

```
200 DIM B (250)
 .
 .
 .
450 ERASE A,B
460 DIM B(3,4)
```

Arrays A and B are eliminated from the program. The B array is redimensioned to a 3-column by 4-row array (12 elements), all of which are set to a zero value.

ERDEV and ERDEV$ Variables

Purpose:

To return the actual value (ERDEV) of a device error, and the name of the device (ERDEV$) causing the error.

Syntax:

ERDEV
ERDEV$

Comments:

ERDEV will contain the error code from interrupt 24H in the lower 8 bits. Bits 8 to 15 from the attribute word in the Device Header Block are mapped directly into the upper 8 bits.

ERDEV$ will contain the 8-byte character device name if the error was on a character device. It will contain the 2-byte block device name (A:, B:, etc.) if the device was not a character device.

Examples:

Installed device driver **lpt2:** caused a "Printer out of paper" error via INT 24H.

ERDEV contains the error number 9 in the lower 8 bits, while the upper 8 bits contain the upper byte of the Device Header word attributes.

```
ERDEV$ contains "LPT2:    ".
```

ERR and ERL Variables

Purpose:

To return the error code (ERR) and line number (ERL) associated with
an error.

Syntax:

v = ERR
v = ERL

Comments:

The variable ERR contains the error code for the last occurrence of an error.
All the error codes and their definitions are listed in Appendix A.

The variable ERL contains the line number of the line in which the error
was detected.

The ERR and ERL Variables are usually used in IF-THEN, or ON
ERROR...GOTO, or GOSUB statements to direct program flow in error
trapping.

If the statement that caused the error was a direct mode statement, ERL
will contain 65535. To test if an error occurred in a direct mode statement,
use a line of the following form:

```
IF 65535=ERL THEN ...
```

Otherwise, use the following:

```
10 IF ERR=error code THEN...GOSUB 4000
20 IF ERL=line number THEN...GOSUB 4010
```

Note

If the line number is not on the right side of the relational operator, it cannot be renumbered by RENUM.

Because ERL and ERR are reserved variables, neither may appear to the left of the equal sign in a LET (assignment) statement.

ERROR Statement

Purpose:

To simulate the occurrence of an error, or to allow the user to define
error codes.

Syntax:

ERROR *integer expression*

Comments:

The value of *integer expression* must be greater than 0 and less than 255.

If the value of *integer expression* equals an error code already in use by
GW-BASIC, the ERROR statement simulates the occurrence of that error,
and the corresponding error message is printed.

A user-defined error code must use a value greater than any used by the
GW-BASIC error codes. There are 76 GW-BASIC error codes at present. It is
preferable to use a code number high enough to remain valid when more
error codes are added to GW-BASIC.

User-defined error codes may be used in an error-trapping routine.

If an ERROR statement specifies a code for which no error message has
been defined, GW-BASIC responds with the message "Unprintable Error."

Execution of an ERROR statement for which there is no error-trapping
routine causes an error message to be printed and execution to halt.

For a complete list of the error codes and messages already defined in
GW-BASIC, refer to Appendix A.

Examples:

The following examples simulate error 15 (the code for "String too long"):

```
LIST
10  S=10
20  T=5
```

```
30 ERROR S+T
40 END
Ok
RUN
String too long in 30
```

Or, in direct mode:

```
Ok
ERROR 15 (you type this line)
String too long (GW-BASIC types this line)
Ok
```

The following example includes a user-defined error code message.

```
        .
        .
        .
110 ON ERROR GOTO 400
120 INPUT "WHAT IS YOUR BET";B
130 IF B>5000 THEN ERROR 210
        .
        .
        .
400 IF ERR=210 THEN PRINT "HOUSE LIMIT IS $5000"
410 IF ERL=130 THEN RESUME 120
        .
        .
        .
```

EXP Function

Purpose:

To return *e* (the base of natural logarithms) to the power of *x*.

Syntax:

EXP(*x*)

Comments:

x must be less than 88.02969.

If EXP overflows, the "Overflow" error message appears; machine infinity with the appropriate sign is supplied as the result, and execution continues.

EXP(*x*) is calculated in single-precision, unless the **/d** switch is used when GW-BASIC is executed.

Examples:

```
10 X = 5
20 PRINT EXP(X-1)
RUN
          54.59815
Ok
```

Prints the value of *e* to the 4th power.

EXTERR Function

Purpose:

To return extended error information.

Syntax:

EXTERR(*n*)

Comments:

EXTERR returns "extended" error information provided by versions of
DOS 3.0 and greater. For versions of DOS earlier than 3.0, EXTERR always
returns zero. The single integer argument must be in the range 0–3
as follows:

Value of *n*	Return Value
0	Extended error code
1	Extended error class
2	Extended error suggested action
3	Extended error locus

The values returned are *not* defined by GW-BASIC, but by DOS. Refer to the
MS-DOS Programmer's Reference (version 3.0 or later) for a description
of the values returned by the DOS extended error function.

The extended error code is actually retrieved and saved by GW-BASIC each
time appropriate DOS functions are performed. Thus, when an EXTERR
function call is made, these saved values are returned.

FIELD Statement

Purpose:

To allocate space for variables in a random file buffer.

Syntax:

FIELD [#] *filenum, width* **AS** *stringvar* [,*width* **AS** *stringvar*]...

Comments:

filenum is the number under which the file was opened.

width is the number of characters to be allocated to the string variable.

string variable is a string variable that will be used for random file access.

A FIELD statement must have been executed before you can

- get data out of a random buffer after a GET statement
- enter data before a PUT statement

For example, the following line allocates the first 20 positions (bytes) in the random file buffer to the string variable N$, the next 10 positions to ID$, and the next 40 positions to ADD$:

```
FIELD 1, 20 AS N$, 10 AS ID$, 40 AS ADD$
```

FIELD only allocates space; it does not place any data in the random file buffer.

The total number of bytes allocated in a FIELD statement must not exceed the record length specified when the file was opened. Otherwise, a "Field overflow" error occurs (the default record length is 128).

Any number of FIELD statements may be executed for the same file, and all FIELD statements executed are in effect at the same time.

Note

Do not use a fielded variable name in an INPUT or LET statement. Once a variable name is fielded, it points to the correct place in the random file buffer. If a subsequent INPUT or LET statement with that variable name is executed, the variable's pointer is moved to string space (see the LSET/RSET and GET statements).

FILES Command

Purpose:

To print the names of the files residing on the specified drive.

Syntax:

FILES [*pathname*]

Comments:

If *pathname* is omitted, the command lists *all* files in the current directory of the selected drive. *pathname* may contain question marks (?) to match any character in the filename or extension. An asterisk (*) as the first character of the filename or extension will match any file or any extension.

This syntax also displays the name of the directory and the number of bytes in the file. When a tree-structured directory is used, two special symbols also appear.

Subdirectories are denoted by <DIR> following the directory name.

Examples:

```
FILES
FILES "*.BAS"
FILES "B:*.*"
FILES "TEST?.BAS"
```

FILES now allows pathnames. The directory for the specified path is displayed. If an explicit path is not given, the current directory is assumed.

```
FILES "ACCTS\"
```

Lists all files in the directory named *accts* that are on the diskette in Drive B: and have the extension of *.pay*.

```
FILES "B:ACCTS\*.PAY"
```

Lists all files in the directory named *accts* that are on the diskette in Drive B: and have the extension of .PAY.

FIX Function

Purpose:

To truncate x to a whole number.

Syntax:

FIX(x)

Comments:

FIX does not round off numbers, it simply eliminates the decimal point and all characters to the right of the decimal point.

FIX(x) is equivalent to SGN(x)*INT(ABS(x)). The major difference between FIX and INT is that FIX does not return the next lower number for negative x.

FIX is useful in modulus arithmetic.

Examples:

```
PRINT FIX(58.75)
        58
Ok

PRINT FIX(-58.75)
       -58
Ok
```

FOR and NEXT Statements

Purpose:

To execute a series of instructions a specified number of times in a loop.

Syntax:

FOR *variable*=*x* **TO** *y* [**STEP** *z*]
.
.
.
NEXT [*variable*][,*variable*...]

Comments:

variable is used as a counter.

x, *y*, and *z* are numeric expressions.

STEP *z* specifies the counter increment for each loop.

The first numeric expression (*x*) is the initial value of the counter. The second numeric expression (*y*) is the final value of the counter.

Program lines following the FOR statement are executed until the NEXT statement is encountered. Then, the counter is incremented by the amount specified by STEP.

If STEP is not specified, the increment is assumed to be 1.

A check is performed to see if the value of the counter is now greater than the final value (*y*). If it is not greater, GW-BASIC branches back to the statement after the FOR statement, and the process is repeated. If it is greater, execution continues with the statement following the NEXT statement. This is a FOR-NEXT loop.

The body of the loop is skipped if the initial value of the loop times the sign of the step exceeds the final value times the sign of the step.

If STEP is negative, the final value of the counter is set to be less than the initial value. The counter is decremented each time through the loop, and the loop is executed until the counter is less than the final value.

Nested Loops

FOR-NEXT loops may be nested; that is, a FOR-NEXT loop may be placed within the context of another FOR-NEXT loop. When loops are nested, each loop must have a unique variable name as its counter.

The NEXT statement for the inside loop must appear before that for the outside loop.

If nested loops have the same end point, a single NEXT statement may be used for all of them.

The *variable(s)* in the NEXT statement may be omitted, in which case the NEXT statement will match the most recent FOR statement.

If a NEXT statement is encountered before its corresponding FOR statement, a "NEXT without FOR" error message is issued and execution is terminated.

Examples:

The following example prints integer values of the variable I% from 1 to 10 in steps of z. For fastest execution, I is declared as an integer by the % sign.

```
10 K=10
20 FOR I%=1 TO K STEP 2
30 PRINT I%
.
.
.
60 NEXT
RUN
 1
 3
 5
 7
 9
Ok
```

FOR and NEXT Statements

In the following example, the loop does not execute because the initial value of the loop exceeds the final value. Nothing is printed by this example.

```
10 R=0
20 FOR S=1 TO R
30 PRINT S
40 NEXT S
```

In the next example, the loop executes 10 times. The final value for the loop variable is always set before the initial value is set.

```
10 S=5
20 FOR S=1 TO S+5
30 PRINT S;
40 NEXT
RUN
          1   2   3   4   5   6   7   8   9   10
Ok
```

FRE Function

Purpose:

To return the number of available bytes in allocated string memory.

Syntax:

FRE(*x*$)
FRE(*x*)

Comments:

Arguments (*x*$) and (*x*) are dummy arguments.

Before FRE (*x*$) returns the amount of space available in allocated string memory, GW-BASIC initiates a "garbage collection" activity. Data in string memory space is collected and reorganized, and unused portions of fragmented strings are discarded to make room for new input.

If FRE is not used, GW-BASIC initiates an automatic garbage collection activity when all string memory space is used up. GW-BASIC will not initiate garbage collection until all free memory has been used. Garbage collection may take 1 to 1.5 minutes.

FRE("") or any string forces a garbage collection before returning the number of free bytes. Therefore, using FRE("") periodically will result in shorter delays for each garbage collection.

It should be noted that the CTRL-BREAK function cannot be used during this housecleaning process.

Examples:

```
PRINT FRE(0)
        14542
Ok
```

Your computer may return a different value.

GET Statement (Files)

Purpose:

To read a record from a random disk file into a random buffer.

Syntax:

GET [#]*file number*[,*record number*]

Comments:

file number is the number under which the file was opened.

record number is the number of the record, within the range of 1 to 16,777,215.

If *record number* is omitted, the next record (after the last GET) is read into the buffer.

After a GET statement, INPUT# and LINE INPUT# may be used to read characters from the random file buffer.

GET may also be used for communications files. *record number* is the number of bytes to be read from the communications buffer. *record number* cannot exceed the buffer length set in the OPEN COM(*n*) statement.

Examples:

The following example opens the vendor file for random access, defines the fields, reads a record, then displays it:

```
10 OPEN "R",1,"A:VENDOR.FIL"
20 FIELD 1,30 AS VENDNAMES$,20 AS ADDR$,15 AS CITY$
30 GET 1
40 PRINT VENDNAMES$,ADDR$,CITY$
50 CLOSE 1
```

This example opens the file *vendor.fil* for random access, with fields defined in line 20. In line 30, the GET statement reads a record into the file buffer. Line 40 displays the information from the record just read. Line 50 closes the file.

144

GET Statement (Graphics)

Purpose:

To transfer graphics images from the screen.

Syntax:

GET (x1,y1)-(x2,y2),*array name*

Comments:

The PUT and GET statements are used to transfer graphics images to and from the screen. PUT and GET make animation and high-speed object motion possible in either graphics mode.

The GET statement transfers the screen image bounded by the rectangle described by the specified points into the array. The rectangle is defined the same way as the rectangle drawn by the LINE statement using the ,**B** option.

The array is used simply as a place to hold the image, and can be of any type except string. It must be dimensioned large enough to hold the entire image. The contents of the array after a GET will be meaningless when interpreted directly (unless the array is of the type integer, as shown below).

The storage format in the array is as follows:

- 2 bytes given x dimension in bits
- 2 bytes given y dimension in bits
- the array data itself

The data for each row of pixels is left-justified on a byte boundary. If less than a multiple of eight bits is stored, the rest of the byte will be filled out with zeros. The required array size in bytes is as follows:

$4 + INT((x*bitsperpixel + 7)/8)*y$

See the SCREEN statement for bitsperpixel values for different screen modes.

The bytes-per-element of an array are as follows:

- 2 for integer
- 4 for single-precision
- 8 for double-precision

The number of bytes required to get a 10 by 12 image into an integer array is $4 + \text{INT}((10*2 + 7)/8)*12$, or 40 bytes. An integer array with at least 20 elements is necessary.

If OPTION BASE equals zero, an integer array can be used to examine the x and y dimensions and the data. The x dimension is in element 0 of the array, and the y dimension is in element 1. Integers are stored low byte first, then high byte, but data is transferred high byte first (leftmost), then low byte.

It is possible to get an image in one mode and put it in another, although the effect may be quite strange because of the way points are represented in each mode.

Examples:

```
10  CLS:SCREEN 1
20  PSET(130,120)
30  DRAW "U25;E7;R20;D32;L6;U12;L14"
40  DRAW "D12;L6":PSET(137,102)
50  DRAW "U4;E4;R8;D8;L12"
60  PSET(137,88)
70  DRAW "E4;R20;D32;G4":PAINT(139,87)
80  DIM A(500)
90  GET (125,130)-(170,80),A
100 FOR I=1 TO 1000:NEXT I
110 PUT (20,20),A,PSET
120 FOR I=1 TO 1000:NEXT I
130 GET (125,130)-(170,80),A
140 FOR I=1 TO 1000:NEXT I
150 PUT (220,130),A,PRESET
```

GOSUB...RETURN Statement

Purpose:

To branch to, and return from, a subroutine.

Syntax:

GOSUB *line number*

.

.

.

RETURN [*line number*]

Comments:

line number is the first line number of the subroutine.

A subroutine may be called any number of times in a program, and a subroutine may be called from within another subroutine. Such nesting of subroutines is limited only by available memory.

A RETURN statement in a subroutine causes GW-BASIC to return to the statement following the most recent GOSUB statement. A subroutine can contain more than one RETURN statement, should logic dictate a RETURN at different points in the subroutine.

Subroutines can appear anywhere in the program, but must be readily distinguishable from the main program.

To prevent inadvertent entry, precede the subroutine by a STOP, END, or GOTO statement to direct program control around the subroutine.

Examples:

```
10 GOSUB 40
20 PRINT "BACK FROM SUBROUTINE"
30 END
40 PRINT "SUBROUTINE";
50 PRINT " IN";
60 PRINT " PROGRESS"
70 RETURN
```

```
RUN
SUBROUTINE IN PROGRESS
BACK FROM SUBROUTINE
Ok
```

The END statement in line 30 prevents re-execution of the subroutine.

GOTO Statement

Purpose:

To branch unconditionally out of the normal program sequence to a specified line number.

Syntax:

GOTO *line number*

Comments:

line number is any valid line number within the program.

If *line number* is an executable statement, that statement and those following are executed. If it is a nonexecutable statement, execution proceeds at the first executable statement encountered after *line number*.

Examples:

```
10  READ R
20  PRINT "R =";R;
30  A = 3.14*R^2
40  PRINT "AREA =";A
50  GOTO 10
60  DATA 5,7,12
RUN
R = 5     AREA = 78.5
R = 7     AREA = 153.86
R = 12    AREA = 452.16
Out of data in 10
Ok
```

The "out of data" advisory is generated when the program attempts to read a fourth DATA statement (which does not exist) in line 60.

HEX$ Function

Purpose:

To return a string that represents the hexadecimal value of the numeric argument.

Syntax:

v$ = **HEX$(x)**

Comments:

HEX$ converts decimal values within the range of -32768 to $+65535$ into a hexadecimal string expression within the range of 0 to FFFF.

Hexadecimal numbers are numbers to the base 16, rather than base 10 (decimal numbers). Appendixes C and G contain more information on hexadecimals and their equivalents.

x is rounded to an integer before HEX$(x) is evaluated. See the OCT$ function for octal conversions.

If x is negative, 2's (binary) complement form is used.

Examples:

```
10 CLS:INPUT "INPUT DECIMAL NUMBER";X
20 A$=HEX$(X)
30 PRINT X "DECIMAL IS "A$" HEXADECIMAL"
RUN
INPUT DECIMAL NUMBER? 32
        32 DECIMAL IS 20 HEXADECIMAL
Ok
```

IF Statement

Purpose:

To make a decision regarding program flow based on the result returned by an expression.

Syntax:

IF *expression*[,] **THEN** *statement(s)*[,][**ELSE** *statement(s)*]
IF *expression*[,] **GOTO** *line number*[[,] **ELSE** *statement(s)*]

Comments:

If the result of *expression* is nonzero (logical true), the THEN or GOTO line number is executed.

If the result of *expression* is zero (false), the THEN or GOTO line number is ignored and the ELSE line number, if present, is executed. Otherwise, execution continues with the next executable statement. A comma is allowed before THEN and ELSE.

THEN and ELSE may be followed by either a line number for branching, or one or more statements to be executed.

GOTO is always followed by a line number.

If the statement does not contain the same number of ELSE's and THEN's line number, each ELSE is matched with the closest unmatched THEN. For example:

```
IF A=B THEN IF B=C THEN PRINT "A=C" ELSE PRINT "A < > C"
```

will not print "A < > C" when A < > B.

If an IF...THEN statement is followed by a line number in the direct mode, an "Undefined line number" error results, unless a statement with the specified line number was previously entered in the indirect mode.

Because IF...THEN...ELSE is all one statement, the ELSE clause cannot be on a separate line. All must be on one line.

Nesting of IF Statements

IF...THEN...ELSE statements may be nested. Nesting is limited only by the length of the line. For example, the following is a legal statement:

```
100 IF X > Y THEN PRINT "GREATER" ELSE IF Y > X THEN&
110   PRINT "LESS THAN"
200 ELSE PRINT "EQUAL"
```

Testing Equality

When using IF to test equality for a value that is the result of a floating-point computation, remember that the internal representation of the value may not be exact. Therefore, test against the range over which the accuracy of the value may vary.

For example, to test a computed variable A against the value 1.0, use the following statement:

```
100 IF ABS (A-1.0)<1.0E-6 THEN ...
```

This test returns true if the value of A is 1.0 with a relative error of less than $1.0E-6$.

Examples:

The following statement gets record number N, if N is not zero.

```
200 IF N THEN GET#1,N
```

In the following example, a test determines if N is greater than 10 and less than 20. If N is within this range, DB is calculated and execution branches to line 300. If N is not within this range, execution continues with line 110.

```
100 IF(N<20) and (N>10) THEN DB=1979-1:GOTO 300
110 PRINT "OUT OF RANGE"
```

The next statement causes printed output to go either to the terminal or to the line printer, depending on the value of a variable (IOFLAG). If IOFLAG is zero, output goes to the line printer; otherwise, output goes to the terminal.

```
210 IF IOFLAG THEN PRINT A$ ELSE LPRINT A$
```

INKEY$ Variable

Purpose:

To return one character read from the keyboard.

Syntax:

v$ = **INKEY$**

Comments:

If no character is pending in the keyboard buffer, a null string (length zero) is returned.

If several characters are pending, only the first is returned. The string will be one or two characters in length.

Two character strings are used to return the extended codes described in Appendix C. The first character of a two character code is zero.

No characters are displayed on the screen, and all characters except the following are passed to the program:

CTRL-BREAK
CTRL-NUM-LOCK
CTRL-ALT-DEL
CTRL-PRTSC
PRTSC

Examples:

```
10 CLS: PRINT"PRESS RETURN
20 TIMELIMIT% = 1000
30 GOSUB 1010
40 IF TIMEOUT% THEN PRINT "TOO LONG" ELSE PRINT "GOOD SHOW"
50 PRINT RESPONSE$
60 END
 .
 .
 .
```

```
1000 REM TIMED INPUT SUBROUTINE
1010 RESPONSE$=""
1020 FOR N%=1 TO TIMELIMIT%
1030 A$=INKEY$:IF LEN(A$)=0 THEN 1060
1040 IF ASC(A$)=13 THEN TIMEOUT%=0:RETURN
1050 RESPONSE$=RESPONSE$+A$
1060 NEXT N%
1070 TIMEOUT%=1:RETURN
```

When this program is executed, and if the RETURN key is pressed before 1000 loops are completed, then "GOOD SHOW" is printed on the screen. Otherwise, "TOO LONG" is printed.

Since an INKEY$ statement scans the keyboard only once, place INKEY$ statements within loops to provide adequate response times for the operator.

INP Function

Purpose:

To return the byte read from machine port n.

Syntax:

INP(n)

Comments:

n represents a valid machine port number within the range of 0 to 65535.

The INP function is one way in which a peripheral device may communicate with a GW-BASIC program.

INP is the complementary function to the OUT statement.

Examples:

```
100 A=INP(56)
```

Upon execution, variable A contains the value present on port 56. The number returned will be within the range of 0 to 255, decimal.

The assembly language equivalent to this statement is

```
MOV DX,56
IN AL,DX
```

INPUT Statement

Purpose:

To prepare the program for input from the terminal during program execution.

Syntax:

INPUT[;][_prompt string_**;]** _list of variables_
INPUT[;][_prompt string_**,]** _list of variables_

Comments:

prompt string is a request for data to be supplied during program execution.

list of variables contains the variable(s) that stores the data in the prompt string.

Each data item in the _prompt string_ must be surrounded by double quotation marks, followed by a semicolon or comma and the name of the variable to which it will be assigned. If more than one _variable_ is given, data items must be separated by commas.

The data entered is assigned to the variable list. The number of data items supplied must be the same as the number of variables in the list.

The variable names in the list may be numeric or string variable names (including subscripted variables). The type of each data item input must agree with the type specified by the variable name.

Too many or too few data items, or the wrong type of values (for example, numeric instead of string), causes the messsage "?Redo from start" to be printed. No assignment of input values is made until an acceptable response is given.

A comma may be used instead of a semicolon after _prompt string_ to suppress the question mark. For example, the following line prints the prompt with no question mark:

```
INPUT    "ENTER BIRTHDATE",B$
```

If the prompt string is preceded by a semicolon, the RETURN key pressed by the operator is suppressed. During program execution, data on that line is displayed, and data from the next PRINT statement is added to the line.

When an INPUT statement is encountered during program execution, the program halts, the prompt string is displayed, and the operator types in the requested data. Strings that input to an INPUT statement need not be surrounded by double quotation marks unless they contain commas or leading or trailing blanks.

When the operator presses the RETURN key, program execution continues.

INPUT and LINE INPUT statements have built-in PRINT statements. When an INPUT statement with a quoted string is encountered during program execution, the quoted string is printed automatically (see the PRINT statement).

The principal difference between the INPUT and LINE INPUT statements is that LINE INPUT accepts special characters (such as commas) within a string, without requiring double quotation marks, while the INPUT statement requires double quotation marks.

Example 1:

To find the square of a number:

```
10 INPUT X
20 PRINT X "SQUARED IS" X^2
30 END
RUN
?
```

The operator types a number (5) in response to the question mark:

```
5 SQUARED IS 25
Ok
```

Example 2:

To find the area of a circle when the radius is known:

```
10 PI=3.14
20 INPUT "WHAT IS THE RADIUS";R
30 A=PI*R^2
```

```
40 PRINT "THE AREA OF THE CIRCLE IS";A
50 PRINT
60 GOTO 20
RUN
WHAT IS THE RADIUS? 7.4
THE AREA OF THE CIRCLE IS 171.9464
```

Note that line 20 in the above example makes use of the built-in PRINT statement contained within INPUT.

INPUT# Statement

Purpose:

To read data items from a sequential file and assign them to program variables.

Syntax:

INPUT# *file number, variable list*

Comments:

file number is the number used when the file was opened for input.

variable list contains the variable names to be assigned to the items in the file.

The data items in the file appear just as they would if data were being typed on the keyboard in response to an INPUT statement.

The variable type must match the type specified by the variable name.

With INPUT#, no question mark is printed, as it is with INPUT.

Numeric Values

For numeric values, leading spaces and line feeds are ignored. The first character encountered (not a space or line feed) is assumed to be the start of a number. The number terminates on a space, carriage return, line feed, or comma.

Strings

If GW-BASIC is scanning the sequential data file for a string, leading spaces and line feeds are ignored.

If the first character is a double quotation mark ("), the string will consist of all characters read between the first double quotation mark and the second. A quoted string may not contain a double quotation mark as a character. The second double quotation mark always terminates the string.

If the first character of the string is not a double quotation mark, the string terminates on a comma, carriage return, or line feed, or after 255 characters have been read.

If the end of the file is reached when a numeric or string item is being INPUT, the item is terminated.

INPUT# can also be used with random files.

INPUT$ Function

Purpose:

To return a string of x characters read from the keyboard, or from file number.

Syntax:

INPUT$(*x*[,[**#**]*file number*)]

Comments:

If the keyboard is used for input, no characters will appear on the screen. All control characters (except CTRL-BREAK) are passed through. CTRL-BREAK interrupts the execution of the INPUT$ function.

The INPUT$ function is preferred over INPUT and LINE INPUT statements for reading communications files, because all ASCII characters may be significant in communications. INPUT is the least desirable because input stops when a comma or carriage return is seen. LINE INPUT terminates when a carriage return is seen.

INPUT$ allows all characters read to be assigned to a string. INPUT$ will return x characters from the file number or keyboard.

For more information about communications, refer to Appendix F.

Example 1:

The following example lists the contents of a sequential file in hexadecimal:

```
10 OPEN"I",1,"DATA"
20 IF EOF(1) THEN 50
30 PRINT HEX$(ASC(INPUT$(1,#1)));
40 GOTO 20
50 PRINT
60 END
```

Example 2:

In the following program, the program pauses, awaiting a keyboard entry of either P or S. Line 130 continues to loop back to line 100 if the input is other than P or S.

```
   .
   .
   .
100 PRINT "TYPE P TO PROCEED OR S TO STOP"
110 X$=INPUT$(1)
120 IF X$="P" THEN 500
130 IF X$="S" THEN 700 ELSE 100
   .
   .
```

INSTR Function

Purpose:

To search for the first occurrence of string y$ in x$, and return the position at which the string is found.

Syntax:

INSTR([*n*,]x$,y$)

Comments:

Optional offset *n* sets the position for starting the search. The default value for *n* is 1.

If *n* equals zero, the error message "Illegal argument in line number" is returned.

n must be within the range of 1 to 255. If *n* is out of this range, an "Illegal Function Call" error is returned.

INSTR returns 0 if

- $n > LEN(x\$)$
- x$ is null
- y$ cannot be found

If y$ is null, INSTR returns *n*.

x$ and y$ may be string variables, string expressions, or string literals.

Examples:

```
10 X$="ABCDEBXYZ"
20 Y$="B"
30 PRINT INSTR(X$,Y$);INSTR(4,X$,Y$)
RUN
        2       6
Ok
```

The interpreter searches the string **"ABCDFBXYZ"** and finds the first occurrence of the character B at position 2 in the string. It then starts another search at position 4 (D) and finds the second match at position 6 (B). The last three characters are ignored, since all conditions set out in line 30 were satisfied.

INT Function

Purpose:

To truncate an expression to a whole number.

Syntax:

INT(*x*)

Comments:

Negative numbers return the next lowest number.

The FIX and CINT functions also return integer values.

Examples:

```
PRINT INT(98.89)
        98
Ok

PRINT INT(-12.11)
-13
Ok
```

IOCTL Statement

Purpose:

To allow GW-BASIC to send a "control data" string to a character device driver anytime after the driver has been opened.

Syntax:

IOCTL[#]file number,string

Comments:

file number is the file number open to the device driver.

string is a valid string expression containing characters that control the device.

IOCTL commands are generally 2 to 3 characters followed by an optional alphanumeric argument. An IOCTL string may be up to 255 bytes long, with commands within the string separated by semicolons.

Examples:

If a user had installed a driver to replace **lpt1**, and that driver was able to set page length (the number of lines to print on a page before issuing a form feed), then the following lines would open the new **lpt1** driver and set the page length to 66 lines:

```
OPEN "LPT1:" FOR OUTPUT AS #1
IOCTL #1,"PL66"
```

The following statements open **lpt1** with an initial page length of 56 lines:

```
OPEN "\DEV\LPT1" FOR OUTPUT AS #1
IOCTL #1,"PL56"
```

IOCTL$ Function

Purpose:

To allow GW-BASIC to read a "control data" string from an open character device driver.

Syntax:

IOCTL$([#]*file number***)**

Comments:

file number is the file number open to the device.

The IOCTL$ function is generally used to get acknowledgment that an IOCTL statement succeeded or failed. It is also used to get device information, such as device width after an IOCTL statement requests it.

Examples:

```
10 'GW is a possible command
20 'for get device width
30 OPEN "\DEV\MYLPT" AS#1
40 IOCTYL#1,"GW"
50 'Save it in WID
60 WID=VAL(IOCTL$(#1))
```

KEY Statement

Purpose:

To allow rapid entry of as many as 15 characters into a program with one keystroke by redefining GW-BASIC special function keys.

Syntax:

KEY *key number,string expression*
KEY *n,***CHR\$**(*hexcode*) + **CHR\$**(*scan code*)
KEY ON
KEY OFF
KEY LIST

Comments:

key number is the number of the key to be redefined. *key number* may range from 1–20.

string expression is the key assignment. Any valid string of 1 to 15 characters may be used. If a string is longer than 15 characters, only the first 15 will be assigned. Constants must be enclosed in double quotation marks.

scan code is the variable defining the key you want to trap. Appendix H lists the scan codes for the keyboard keys.

hexcode is the hexadecimal code assigned to the key shown below:

Key	Hexcode
EXTENDED	&H80
CAPS LOCK	&H40
NUM LOCK	&H20
ALT	&H08
CTRL	&H04
SHIFT	&H01, &H02, &H03

Hexcodes may be added together, such as in &H03, which is both shift keys.

Initially, the function keys are assigned the following special functions:

F1	LIST	F2	RUN<-
F3	LOAD"	F4	SAVE"
F5	CONT<-	F6	,"LPT1:"<-
F7	TRON<-	F8	TROFF<-
F9	KEY	F10	SCREEN 000<-

Note

    <- (arrow) means that you do not have to press RETURN after each of these keys has been pressed.

Any one or all of the 10 keys may be redefined. When the key is pressed, the data assigned to it will be input to the program.

```
KEY key number,"string expression"
```

Assigns the string expression to the specified key.

```
KEY LIST
```

Lists all 10 key values on the screen. All 15 characters of each value are displayed.

```
KEY ON
```

Displays the first six characters of the key values on the 25th line of the screen. When the display width is set at 40, five of the 10 keys are displayed. When the width is set at 80, all 10 are displayed.

```
KEY OFF
```

Erases the key display from the 25th line, making that line available for program use. KEY OFF does not disable the function keys.

If the value for *key number* is not within the range of 1 to 10, or 15 to 20, an "Illegal function call" error occurs. The previous KEY assignment is retained.

Assigning a null string (length 0) disables the key as a function key.

When a function key is redefined, the INKEY$ function returns one character of the assigned string per invocation. If the function key is disabled, INKEY$ returns a string of two characters: the first is binary zero; the second is the key scan code.

Examples:

```
10 KEY 1,"MENU"+CHR$(13)
```

Displays a menu selected by the operator each time key 1 is pressed.

```
1 KEY OFF
```

Turns off the key display.

```
10 DATA KEY1,KEY2,KEY3,KEY4,KEY5
20 FOR N=1 TO 5:READ SOFTKEYS$(n)
30 KEY N,SOFTKEYS$(I)
40 NEXT N
50 KEY ON
```

Displays new function keys on line 25 of the screen.

```
20 KEY 1,""
```

Disables function key 1.

KEY(n) Statement

Purpose:

To initiate and terminate key capture in a GW-BASIC program.

Syntax:

KEY(*n*) **ON**
KEY(*n*) **OFF**
KEY(*n*) **STOP**

Comments:

n is a number from 1 to 20 that indicates which key is to be captured. Keys are numbered as follows:

Key Number	Key
1–10	Function keys F1 through F10
11	CURSOR-UP
12	CURSOR-LEFT
13	CURSOR-RIGHT
14	CURSOR-DOWN
15–20	Keys defined in the following format (see KEY statement): KEY *n*,CHR$(*hexcode*) + CHR$(*scan code*)

Execution of the KEY(*n*) ON statement is required to activate keystroke capture from the function keys or cursor control keys. When the KEY(*n*) ON statement is activated and enabled, GW-BASIC checks each new statement to see if the specified key is pressed. If so, GW-BASIC performs a GOSUB to the line number specified in the ON KEY(*n*) statement. An ON KEY(*n*) statement must precede a KEY(*n*) statement.

When KEY(*n*) OFF is executed, no key capture occurs and no keystrokes are retained.

KEY(n) Statement

If KEY(n) STOP is executed, no key capture occurs, but if a specified key is pressed, the keystroke is retained so that immediate keystroke capture occurs when a KEY(n) ON is executed.

For further information on key trapping, see the ON KEY (n) statement.

KILL Command

Purpose:

To delete a file from a disk.

Syntax:

KILL *filename*

Comments:

filename can be a program file, sequential file, or random-access data file.

KILL is used for all types of disk files, including program, random data, and sequential data files.

Note

> You must specify the filename's extension when using the KILL command. Remember that files saved in GW-BASIC are given the default extension *.bas*.

If a KILL command is given for a file that is currently open, a "File already open" error occurs.

Examples:

The following command deletes the GW-BASIC file *data*, and makes the space available for reallocation to another file:

```
200 KILL "DATA1.BAS"
```

The following command deletes the GW-BASIC file *raining* from the subdirectory *dogs*:

```
KILL "CATS\DOGS\RAINING.BAS"
```

LEFT$ Function

Purpose:

To return a string that comprises the leftmost n characters of x$.

Syntax:

LEFT$(x$,n)

Comments:

n must be within the range of 0 to 255. If n is greater than LEN(x$), the entire string (x$) will be returned. If n equals zero, the null string (length zero) is returned (see the MID$ and RIGHT$ substring functions).

Examples:

```
10 A$="BASIC"
20 B$=LEFT$(A$,3)
30 PRINT B$
RUN
BAS
Ok
```

The leftmost three letters of the string "BASIC" are printed on the screen.

LEN Function

Purpose:

To return the number of characters in x$.

Syntax:

LEN(x$)

Comments:

Nonprinting characters and blanks are counted.

Examples:

x$ is any string expression.

```
10 X$="PORTLAND, OREGON"
20 PRINT LEN(X$)
16
Ok
```

Note that the comma and space are included in the character count of 16.

LET Statement

Purpose:

To assign the value of an expression to a variable.

Syntax:

[LET] *variable = expression*

Comments:

The word LET is optional; that is, the equal sign is sufficient when assigning an expression to a variable name.

The LET statement is seldom used. It is included here to ensure compatibility with previous versions of BASIC that require it.

When using LET, remember that the type of the variable and the type of the expression must match. If they don't, a "Type mismatch" error occurs.

Example 1:

The following example lets you have downward compatibility with an older system. If this downward compatibility is not required, use the second example, as it requires less memory.

```
110 LET D=12
120 LET E=12^2
130 LET F=12^4
140 LET SUM=D+E+F
  .
  .
  .
```

Example 2:

```
110  D=12
120  E=12^2
130  F=12^4
140  SUM=D+E+F
 .
 .
 .
```

LINE Statement

Purpose:

To draw lines and boxes on the screen.

Syntax:

LINE [$(x1,y1)$] – $(x2,y2)$ [,[*attribute*][,**B**[**F**]][,*style*]]

Comments:

x1,y1 and *x2,y2* specify the end points of a line.

Resolution mode is determined by the SCREEN statement.

attribute specifies color or intensity of the displayed pixel (see the COLOR and PALETTE statements).

B (box) draws a box with the points $(x1,y1)$ and $(x2,y2)$ at opposite corners.

BF (filled box) draws a box (as **,B**) and fills in the interior with points.

Note

    If *attribute* is not specified, two commas must be used before **B** or **BF**.

LINE supports the additional argument *style*. *style* is a 16-bit integer mask used when putting down pixels on the screen. This is called *line-styling*.

Each time LINE stores a point on the screen, it uses the current circulating bit in style. If that bit is 0, no store will be done. If the bit is 1, then a normal store is done. After each point, the next bit position in *style* is selected.

Since a 0 bit in *style* does not clear out the old contents, you may wish to draw a background line before a styled line, in order to force a known background.

style is used for normal lines and boxes, but is illegal for filled boxes.

If the **BF** parameter is used with the *style* parameter, a "Syntax" error will occur.

When out-of-range values are given in the LINE statement, the coordinates that are out of range are not visible on the screen. This is called *line-clipping*.

In the syntax shown here, the coordinate form STEP (*x offset,y offset*) is not shown. However, this form can be used wherever a coordinate is used.

In a LINE statement, if the relative form is used on the second coordinate, it is relative to the first coordinate.

After a LINE statement, the last referenced point is *x2,y2*.

The simplest form of LINE is the following:

LINE $-(xz,yz)$

This draws a line from the last point referenced to the point (*xz,yz*) in the foreground color.

Examples:

LINE (0,100)-(639,100)

Draws a horizontal line that divides the screen in half from top to bottom in SCREEN 2.

LINE (160,0)-(160,199)

Draws a vertical line that divides the screen in half from left to right in SCREEN 1; makes a one-quarter/three-quarter division in SCREEN 2.

LINE (0,0)-(319,199)

Draws a diagonal line from the top left to lower right corner of the screen in SCREEN 1, and from the upper left corner to the center bottom of the screen in SCREEN 2.

LINE Statement

```
LINE (10,10)-(20,20),2
```

Draws a line in color 2 if SCREEN 1 was previously specified (see the COLOR statement).

```
10 CLS
20 LINE -(RND*319,RND*199),RND*4
30 GOTO 20
```

Draws lines forever using random attributes.

```
10 FOR X=0 TO 319
20 LINE (X,0)-(X,199),X AND 1
30 NEXT
```

Draws an alternating pattern: line on, line off.

```
10 CLS
20 LINE -(RND*639,RND*199),RND*2,BF
30 GOTO 20
```

Draws lines all over the screen.

```
LINE (0,0)-(100,175),,B
```

Draws a square box in the upper left corner of the screen.

```
LINE (0,0)-(100,175),,BF
```

Draws the same box and fills it in.

```
LINE (0,0)-(100,175),2,BF
```

Draws the same filled box in magenta in SCREEN 1.

```
LINE (0,0)-(100,350),,B
```

Draws the same box if SCREEN 2 is specified.

```
400 SCREEN 1
410 LINE(160,100)-(160,199),,,&HCCCC
```

Draws a vertical dotted line down the center of the screen in SCREEN 1.

```
220 SCREEN 2
230 LINE(300,100)-(400,50),,B,&HAAAA
```

Draws a rectangle with a dotted line in SCREEN 2.

```
LINE (0,0)-(160,100),3,,&HFF00
```

Draws a dotted line from the upper left corner to the screen center.

LINE INPUT Statement

Purpose:

To input an entire line (up to 255 characters) from the keyboard into a string variable, ignoring delimiters.

Syntax:

LINE INPUT [;][*prompt string;*]*string variable*

Comments:

prompt string is a string literal, displayed on the screen, that allows user input during program execution.

A question mark is not printed unless it is part of *prompt string*.

string variable accepts all input from the end of the prompt to the carriage return. Trailing blanks are ignored.

LINE INPUT is almost the same as the INPUT statement, except that it accepts special characters (such as commas) in operator input during program execution.

If a line-feed/carriage return sequence (this order only) is encountered, both characters are input and echoed. Data input continues.

If LINE INPUT is immediately followed by a semicolon, pressing the RETURN key will not move the cursor to the next line.

A LINE INPUT may be escaped by typing CTRL-BREAK. GW-BASIC returns to command level and displays *Ok*.

Typing CONT resumes execution at the LINE INPUT line.

Example:

```
100 LINE INPUT A$
```

Program execution pauses at line 100, and all keyboard characters typed thereafter are input to string A$ until RETURN, CTRL-M, CTRL-C, or CTRL-BREAK is entered.

LINE INPUT# Statement

Purpose:

To read an entire line (up to 255 characters), without delimiters, from a sequential disk file to a string variable.

Syntax:

LINE INPUT# *file number, string variable*

Comments:

file number is the number under which the file was opened.

string variable is the variable name to which the line will be assigned.

LINE INPUT# reads all characters in the sequential file up to a carriage return. If a line feed/carriage return sequence (this order only) is encountered, it is input.

LINE INPUT# is especially useful if each line of a data file has been broken into fields, or if a GW-BASIC program saved in ASCII mode is being read as data by another program.

Examples:

```
10 OPEN "O",1,"INFO"
20 LINE INPUT "CUSTOMER INFORMATION?";C$
30 PRINT#1, C$
40 CLOSE 1
50 OPEN "I",1,"INFO"
60 LINE INPUT#1, C$
70 PRINT C$
80 CLOSE 1
RUN
CUSTOMER INFORMATION?
```

If the operator enters

```
LINDA JONES    234,4   MEMPHIS
```

then the program continues with the following:

```
LINDA JONES     234,4    MEMPHIS
Ok
```

LIST Command

Purpose:

To list all or part of a program to the screen, line printer, or file.

Syntax:

LIST [*linenumber*][*-linenumber*][*,filename*]
LIST [*linenumber-*][*,filename*]

Comments:

linenumber is a valid line number within the range of 0 to 65529.

If *filename* is omitted, the specified lines are listed to the screen.

Use the hyphen to specify a line range. If the line range is omitted, the entire program is listed. *linenumber-* lists that line and all higher numbered lines. *-linenumber* lists lines from the beginning of the program through the specified line.

The period (.) can replace either *linenumber* to indicate the current line.

Any listing may be interrupted by pressing CTRL-BREAK.

Examples:

LIST

Lists all lines in the program.

LIST -20

Lists lines 1 through 20.

LIST 10-20

Lists lines 10 through 20.

LIST 20-

Lists lines 20 through the end of the program.

LLIST Command

Purpose:

To list all or part of the program currently in memory to the line printer.

Syntax:

LLIST [*linenumber*][*-linenumber*]
LLIST [*linenumber-*]

Comments:

GW-BASIC always returns to command level after a LLIST is executed. The line range options for LLIST are the same as for LIST.

Examples:

See the examples in the LIST statement.

LOAD Command

Purpose:

To load a file from diskette into memory.

Syntax:

LOAD *filename*[,**r**]

Comments:

filename is the filename used when the file was saved. If the extension was omitted, *.bas* will be used.

LOAD closes all open files and deletes all variables and program lines currently residing in memory before it loads the designated program.

If the **r** option is used with LOAD, the program runs after it is loaded, and all open data files are kept open.

LOAD with the **r** option lets you chain several programs (or segments of the same program). Information can be passed between the programs using the disk data files.

Examples:

```
LOAD "STRTRK",R
```

Loads the file *strtrk.bas* and runs it, retaining all open files and variables from a previous program intact.

189

LOC Function

Purpose:

To return the current position in the file.

Syntax:

LOC(*file number*)

Comments:

file number is the file number used when the file was opened.

When transmitting or receiving a file through a communications port, LOC returns the number of characters in the input buffer waiting to be read. The default size for the input buffer is 256 characters, but can be changed with the /c: option on the GW-BASIC command line. If there are more than 255 characters in the buffer, LOC returns 255. Since a string is limited to 255 characters, this practical limit alleviates the need to test for string size before reading data into it. If fewer than 255 characters remain in the buffer, then LOC returns the actual count.

With random disk files, LOC returns the record number just read from, or written to, with a GET or PUT statement.

With sequential files, LOC returns the number of 128-byte blocks read from, or written to, the file since it was opened. When the sequential file is opened for input, GW-BASIC initially reads the first sector of the file. In this case, the LOC function returns the character *1* before any input is allowed.

If the file was opened but no disk input/output was performed, LOC returns a zero.

Examples:

```
200 IF LOC(1)#50 THEN STOP
```

The program stops after 51 records are read or written.

LOCATE Statement

Purpose:

To move the cursor to the specified position on the active screen. Optional parameters cause the cursor to blink on and off, and define the start and stop *raster lines* for the cursor. A raster line is the vertical or horizontal distance between two adjacent, addressable points on your screen.

Syntax:

LOCATE [*row*][,[*col*][,[*cursor*][,[*start*] [,*stop*]]]]

Comments:

row is the screen line number, a numeric expression within the range of 1 to 25.

col is the screen column number, a numeric expression within the range of 1 to 40, or 1 to 80, depending upon screen width.

cursor is a boolean value indicating whether the cursor is visible; zero is off, nonzero is on.

start is the cursor start scan line, a numeric expression within the range of 0 to 31.

stop is the cursor stop scan line, a numeric expression within the range of 0 to 31.

When the cursor is moved to the specified position, subsequent PRINT statements begin placing characters at this location. Optionally, the LOCATE statement may be used to start the cursor blinking on or off, or change the size of the blinking cursor.

Any values entered outside of these ranges results in "Illegal function call" errors. Previous values are retained.

As you set up the parameters for the LOCATE statement, you may find that you do not wish to change one or more of the existing specifications. To omit a parameter from this LOCATE statement, insert a comma for the parameter that is being skipped. If the omitted parameter(s) occurs at the end of the statement, you do not have to type the comma.

191

If the start scan line parameter is given and the stop scan line parameter is omitted, stop assumes the start value.

Examples:

```
10 LOCATE 1,1
```

Moves the cursor to the home position in the upper left corner.

```
20 LOCATE ,,1
```

Makes the cursor visible. Its position remains unchanged. Notice that the first two parameters are not used. A comma has been inserted for each omitted parameter.

```
30 LOCATE ,,,7
```

Cursor position and visibility remain unchanged. Sets the cursor to appear at the bottom of the character starting and ending on scan line 7.

```
40 LOCATE 5,1,1,0,7
```

Moves the cursor to line 5, column 1, and turns the cursor on. The cursor covers an entire character cell, starting at scan line 0 and ending on scan line 7.

LOCK Statement

Purpose:

To restrict the access to all or part of a file that has been opened by another process. This is used in a multi-device environment, often referred to as a *network* or *network environment*.

Syntax:

LOCK [**#**]*n* [,[*record number*] [**TO** *record number*]]

Comments:

n is the number that was assigned to the file as it was originally numbered in the program.

record number is the number of the individual record that is to be locked. Or, if a range of records are to be locked, *record number* designates the beginning and ending record of the specified range.

The range of legal record numbers is 1 to $2^{32} - 1$. The limit on record size is 32767 bytes.

The record range specified must be from lower to (the same or) higher record numbers.

If a starting record number is not specified, the record number 1 is assumed.

If an ending record number is not specified, then only the specified record is locked.

The following are examples of legal LOCK statements:

LOCK #*n*	locks the entire file *n*
LOCK #*n*, *X*	locks record *X* only
LOCK #*n*, TO *Y*	locks records 1 through *Y*
LOCK #*n*, *X* TO *Y*	locks records *X* through *Y*

With a random-access file, the entire opened file, or a range of records within an opened file, may be locked, thus denying access to those records to any other process that has also opened the file.

With a sequential access file that has been opened for input or output, the entire file is locked, regardless of any record range specified. This is not considered an error. The specification of a range in the LOCK statement regarding the sequential file will simply be disregarded.

The LOCK statement should be executed on a file or record range within a file before attempting to read or write to that file.

The locked file or record range should be unlocked before the file is closed. Failure to execute the UNLOCK statement can jeopardize future access to that file in a network environment.

It is expected that the time in which files or regions within files are locked will be short, and thus the suggested usage of the LOCK statement is within short-term paired LOCK/UNLOCK statements.

Examples:

The following sequence demonstrates how the LOCK/UNLOCK statements should be used:

```
LOCK #1, 1 TO 4
LOCK #1, 5 TO 8
UNLOCK #1, 1 TO 4
UNLOCK #1, 5 TO 8
```

The following example is illegal:

```
LOCK #1, 1 TO 4
LOCK #1, 5 TO 8
UNLOCK #1, 1 TO 8
```

LOF Function

Purpose:

To return the length (number of bytes) allocated to the file.

Syntax:

LOF(*file number*)

Comments:

file number is the number of the file that the file was opened under.

With communications files, LOF returns the amount of free space in the input buffers.

Examples:

The following sequence gets the last record of the random-access file *file.big*, and assumes that the file was created with a default record length of 128 bytes:

```
10 OPEN "R",1,"FILE.BIG"
20 GET #1,LOF(1)/128
 .
 .
 .
```

LOG Function

Purpose:

To return the natural logarithm of x.

Syntax:

LOG(x)

Comments:

x must be a number greater than zero.

LOG(x) is calculated in single-precision, unless the **/d** switch is used when GW-BASIC is executed.

Examples:

```
PRINT LOG(2)
.6931471

PRINT LOG(1)
0
```

LPOS Function

Purpose:

To return the current position of the line printer print head within the line printer buffer.

Syntax:

LPOS(x)

Comments:

LPOS does not necessarily give the physical position of the print head.

x is a dummy argument.

If the printer has less than the 132 characters-per-line capability, it may issue internal line feeds and not inform the computer internal line printer buffer. If this has happened, the value returned by LPOS(x) may be incorrect. LPOS(x) simply counts the number of printable characters since the last line feed was issued.

Examples:

The following line causes a carriage return after the 60th character is printed on a line:

```
100 IF LPOS(X)#60 THEN LPRINT CHR$(13)
```

LPRINT and LPRINT USING Statements

Purpose:

To print data at the line printer.

Syntax:

LPRINT [*list of expressions*][;]
LPRINT USING *string exp*; *list of expressions*[;]

Comments:

list of expressions consists of the string or numeric expression separated by semicolons.

string expressions is a string literal or variable consisting of special formatting characters. The formating characters determine the field and the format of printed strings or numbers.

These statements are the same as PRINT and PRINT USING, except that output goes to the line printer. For more information about string and numeric fields and the variables used in them, see the PRINT and PRINT USING statements.

The LPRINT and LPRINT USING statements assume that your printer is an 80-character-wide printer.

To reset the number of characters that you can print across the printed page (assuming that your printer is wider than 80 characters), see the WIDTH statement.

LSET and RSET Statements

Purpose:

To move data from memory to a random-file buffer and left- or right-justify it in preparation for a PUT statement.

Syntax:

LSET *string variable = string expression*
RSET *string variable = string expression*

Comments:

If *string expression* requires fewer bytes than were fielded to *string variable*, LSET left-justifies the string in the field, and RSET right-justifies the string (spaces are used to pad the extra positions).

If the string is too long for the field, characters are dropped from the right.

To convert numeric values to strings before the LSET or RSET statement is used, see the MKI$, MKS$, and MKD$ functions.

LSET or RSET may also be used with a nonfielded string variable to left-justify or right-justify a string in a given field.

Examples:

```
110 A$=SPACE$(20)
120 RSET A$=N$
```

These two statements right-justify the string N$ in a 20-character field. This can be valuable for formatting printed output.

MERGE Command

Purpose:

To merge the lines from an ASCII program file into the program already in memory.

Syntax:

MERGE *filename*

Comments:

filename is a valid string expression containing the filename. If no extension is specified, then GW-BASIC assumes an extension of *.bas*.

The diskette is searched for the named file. If found, the program lines on the diskette are merged with the lines in memory. After the MERGE command, the merged program resides in memory, and GW-BASIC returns to the direct mode.

If the program being merged was not saved in ASCII code with the **a** option to the SAVE command, a "Bad file mode" error is issued. The program in memory remains unchanged.

If any line numbers in the file have the same number as lines in the program in memory, the lines from the file replace the corresponding lines in memory.

Examples:

```
MERGE "SUBRTN"
```

Merges the file *subrtn.bas* with the program currently in memory, provided *subrtn* was previously saved with the **a** option. If some of the program lines are the same as those in the *subrtn.bas* file being merged, then the original program lines are replaced by the lines from *subrtn.bas*.

MID$ Function

Purpose:

To return a string of *m* characters from v$, beginning with the *n*th character.

Syntax:

MID$(x$,*n*[,*m*])

Comments:

n must be within the range of 1 to 255.

m must be within the range of 0 to 255.

If *m* is omitted, or if there are fewer than *m* characters to the right of *n*, all rightmost characters beginning with *n* are returned.

If *n*>LEN(x$), the MID$ function returns a null string.

If *m* equals 0, the MID$ function returns a null string.

If either *n* or *m* is out of range, an "Illegal function call error" is returned.

For more information and examples, see the LEFT$ and RIGHT$ functions.

Examples:

```
10 A$="GOOD"
20 B$="MORNING EVENING AFTERNOON"
30 PRINT A$;MID$(B$,8,8)
RUN
GOOD EVENING
Ok
```

Line 30 concatenates (joins) the A$ string to another string with a length of eight characters, beginning at position 8 within the B$ string.

MID$ Statement

Purpose:

To replace a portion of one string with another string.

Syntax:

MID$(*stringexp1*,*n*[,*m*]) = *stringexp2*

Comments:

Both *n* and *m* are integer expressions.

stringexp1 and *stringexp2* are string expressions.

The characters in *stringexp1*, beginning at position *n*, are replaced by the characters in *stringexp2*.

The optional *m* refers to the number of characters from *stringexp2* that are used in the replacement. If *m* is omitted, all of *stringexp2* is used.

Whether *m* is omitted or included, the replacement of characters never goes beyond the original length of *stringexp1*.

Examples:

```
10 A$="KANSAS CITY, MO"
20 MID$(A$,14)="KS"
30 PRINT A$
RUN
KANSAS CITY, KS
Ok
```

Line 20 overwrites "MO" in the A$ string with "KS".

MKDIR Command

Purpose:

To create a subdirectory.

Syntax:

MKDIR *pathname*

Comments:

pathname is a string expression, not exceeding 63 characters, identifying the subdirectory to be created.

Examples:

MKDIR "C:SALES\JOHN"

Creates the subdirectory *john* within the directory *sales*.

MKI$, MKS$, MKD$ Functions

Purpose:

To convert numeric values to string values.

Syntax:

MKI$(*integer expression*)
MKS$(*single-precision expression*)
MKD$(*double-precision expression*)

Comments:

MKI$ converts an integer to a 2-byte string.

MKS$ converts a single-precision number to a 4-byte string.

MKD$ converts a double-precision number to an 8-byte string.

Any numeric value placed in a random file buffer with an LSET or a RSET statement must be converted to a string (see CVI, CVS, CVD for the complementary functions).

These functions differ from STR$ because they change the interpretations of the bytes, not the bytes themselves.

Examples:

```
90  AMT=(K+T)
100 FIELD #1,8 AS D$,20 AS N$
110 LSET D$=MKS$(AMT)
120 LSET N$=A$
130 PUT #1
 .
 .
 .
```

NAME Command

Purpose:

To change the name of a disk file.

Syntax:

NAME *old filename* **AS** *new filename*

Comments:

old filename must exist and *new filename* must not exist; otherwise, an error results.

After a NAME command, the file exists on the same diskette, in the same disk location, with the new name.

Examples:

```
NAME "ACCTS" AS "LEDGER"
Ok
```

The file formerly named *accts* will now be named *ledger*. The file content and physical location on the diskette is unchanged.

NEW Command

Purpose:

To delete the program currently in memory and clear all variables.

Syntax:

NEW

Comments:

NEW is entered at command level to clear memory before entering a new program. GW-BASIC always returns to command level after a NEW is executed.

Examples:

```
NEW
OK
```

or

```
980 PRINT "Do You Wish To Quit (Y/N)
990 ANS$=INKEY$: IF ANS$=""THEN 990
1000 IF ANS$="Y" THEN NEW
1010 IF ANS$="N" THEN 980
1020 GOTO 990
```

OCT$ Function

Purpose:

To convert a decimal value to an octal value.

Syntax:

OCT$(*x*)

Comments:

x is rounded to an integer before OCT$(*x*) is evaluated.

This statement converts a decimal value within the range of -32768 to $+65535$ to an octal string expression.

Octal numbers are numbers to base 8 rather than base 10 (decimal numbers).

See the HEX$ function for hexadecimal conversion.

Examples:

```
10 PRINT OCT$(18)
RUN
22
Ok
```

Decimal 18 equals octal 22.

ON COM(n), ON KEY(n), ON PEN, ON PLAY(n), ON STRIG(n), and ON TIMER(n) Statements

Purpose:

To create an event trap line number for a specified event (such as communications, pressing function or cursor control keys, using the light pen, or using joysticks).

Syntax:

ON *event specifier* GOSUB *line number*

Comments:

The syntax shown sets up an event trap line number for the specified event. A *line number* of 0 disables trapping for this event.

Once trap line numbers have been set, event trapping itself can be controlled with the following syntax lines:

event specifier **ON**	When an event is ON, and a nonzero line number is specified for the trap, then every time BASIC starts a new statement, it checks to see if the specified event has occurred. If it has, BASIC performs a GOSUB to the line specified in the ON statement.
event specifier **OFF**	When an event is OFF, no trapping occurs and the event is not remembered, even if it occurs.
event specifier **STOP**	When an event is stopped, no trapping can occur, but if the event happens, it is remembered so an immediate trap occurs when an event specifier ON is executed.

When a trap is made for a particular event, the trap automatically causes a stop on that event, so recursive traps can never take place.

The return from the trap routine automatically does an ON unless an explicit OFF has been performed inside the trap routine.

When an error trap takes place, this automatically disables all trapping.

Trapping will never take place when BASIC is not executing a program.

The following are valid values for *event specifier*:

COM(*n*)	*n* is the number of the COM channel (1 or 2).
KEY(*n*)	*n* is a function key number 1–20. 1 through 10 are the function keys F1 through F10. 11 through 14 are the cursor control keys as follows:

                     11 = Cursor Up   13 = Cursor Right

                     12 = Cursor Left   14 = Cursor Down

                     15–20 are user-defined keys.

PEN	Since there is only one pen, no number is given.
PLAY(*n*)	*n* is an integer expression in the range of 1–32. Values outside this range result in "Illegal function call" errors.
STRIG(*n*)	*n* is 0, 2, 4, or 6. (0 = trigger A1; 4 = trigger A2; 2 = trigger B1; 6 = trigger B2).
TIMER(*n*)	*n* is a numeric expression within the range of 1 to 86,400. A value outside of this range results in an "Illegal function call" error.
RETURN *line number*	This optional form of RETURN is primarily intended for use with event trapping. The event-trapping routine may want to go back into the GW-BASIC program at a fixed line number while still eliminating the GOSUB entry that the trap created.

Use of the nonlocal RETURN must be done with care. Any other GOSUB, WHILE, or FOR that was active at the time of the trap remains active.

If the trap comes out of a subroutine, any attempt to continue loops outside the subroutine results in a "NEXT without FOR" error.

Special Notes About Each Type of Trap

COM Trapping

Typically, the COM trap routine will read an entire message from the COM port before returning.

It is recommended that you not use the COM trap for single character messages, since at high baud rates the overhead of trapping and reading for each individual character may allow the interrupt buffer for COM to overflow.

KEY Trapping

Trappable keys 15 to 20 are defined by the following statement:

KEY(*n*),**CHR$**[*hexcode*] + **CHR$**[*scan code*]

n is an integer expression within the range of 15 to 20 defining the key to be trapped.

hexcode is the mask for the latched key: (CAPS LOCK, NUM LOCK, ALT, CTRL, LEFT SHIFT, RIGHT SHIFT)

scan code is the number identifying one of the 83 keys to trap. Refer to Appendix H for key scan codes.

The appropriate bit in *hexcode* must be set in order to trap a key that is shifted, control-shifted, or alt-shifted. *hexcode* values are as follows:

Mask	Hexcode	Indicates that
EXTENDED	&H80	Key is extended
CAPS LOCK	&H40	CAPS LOCK is active
NUM LOCK	&H20	NUM LOCK is active
ALT	&H08	The ALT key is pressed
CTRL	&H04	The CTRL key is pressed
LEFT SHIFT	&H02	The left SHIFT key is pressed
RIGHT SHIFT	&H01	The right SHIFT key is pressed

For trapping shifted keys, you may use the value &H01, &H02, or &H03. The left and right SHIFT keys are coupled when &H03 is used.

Refer to the KEY(n) statement for more information.

No type of trapping is activated when GW-BASIC is in direct mode. Function keys resume their standard expansion meaning during input.

A key that causes a trap is not available for examination with the INPUT or INKEY$ statement, so the trap routine for each key must be different if a different function is desired.

If CTRL-PRTSC is trapped, the line printer echo toggle is processed first. Defining CTRL-PRTSC as a key trap does not prevent characters from being echoed to the printer if CTRL-PRTSC is pressed.

Function keys 1 through 14 are predefined. Therefore, setting scan codes 59–68, 72, 75, 77, or 80 has no effect.

PLAY(n) Trapping

A PLAY event trap is issued only when playing background music (PLAY"MB..). PLAY event music traps are not issued when running in MUSIC foreground (default case, or PLAY"MF..).

Choose conservative values for n. An ON PLAY(32).. statement will cause event traps so often that there will be little time to execute the rest of your program.

The ON PLAY(n) statement causes an event trap when the background music queue goes from n to n − 1 notes.

STRIG Trapping

Using STRIG(n) ON activates the interrupt routine that checks the trigger status. Downstrokes that cause trapping will not set STRIG(0), STRIG(2), STRIG(4), or STRIG(6) functions.

TIMER(*n*) Trapping

An ON TIMER(*n*) event trapping statement is used with applications needing an internal timer. The trap occurs when *n* seconds have elapsed since the TIMER ON statement.

Example 1:

This is a very simple terminal program.

```
10 REM "ON COM(n)" EXAMPLE
20 OPEN "COM1:9600,0,7" AS #1
30 ON COM(1) GOSUB 80
40 COM(1) ON
50 REM TRANSMIT CHARACTERS FROM KEYBOARD
60 A$=INKEY$:IF A$=""THEN 50
70 PRINT #1,A$;:GOTO 50
80 REM DISPLAY RECEIVE CHARACTERS
90 ALL=LOC(1):IF ALL<1 THEN RETURN
100 B$=INPUT$(ALL,#1):PRINT B$;:RETURN
```

Example 2:

Prevents a CTRL-BREAK or system reset during a program.

```
10 KEY 15,CHR$(4)+CHR$(70) REM Trap ^BREAK
20 KEY 16,CHR$(12)+CHR$(83) REM Trap system reset
30 ON KEY(15) GOSUB 1000
40 ON KEY(16) GOSUB 2000
50 KEY(15) ON
60 KEY(16) ON
    .
    .
    .
1000 PRINT "I'm sorry, I can't let you do that"
1010 RETURN
2000 ATTEMPS=ATTEMPS+1
2010 ON ATTEMPS GOTO 2100,2200,2300,2400,2500
2100 PRINT "Mary had a little lamb":RETURN
2200 PRINT "Its fleece was white as snow":RETURN
2300 PRINT "And everywhere that Mary went":RETURN
2400 PRINT "The lamb was sure to go":RETURN
2500 KEY(16) OFF REM If they hit us once more...
2510 RETURN REM then BASIC dies...
```

Example 3:

Displays the time of day on line 1 every minute.

```
10 ON TIMER(60) GOSUB 10000
20 TIMER ON
   .
   .
   .
10000 OLDROW=CSRLIN REM Saves the current row
10010 OLDCOL=POS(0) REM Saves the current column
10020 LOCATE 1,1:PRINT TIME$
10030 LOCATE OLDROW,OLDCOL REM Restores row and column
10040 RETURN
```

ON ERROR GOTO Statement

Purpose:

To enable error trapping and specify the first line of the error-handling subroutine.

Syntax:

ON ERROR GOTO *line number*

Comments:

Once error trapping has been enabled, all errors detected by GW-BASIC, including direct mode errors (for example, syntax errors), cause GW-BASIC to branch to the line in the program that begins the specified error-handling subroutine.

GW-BASIC branches to the line specified by the ON ERROR statement until a RESUME statement is found.

If *line number* does not exist, an "Undefined line" error results.

To disable error trapping, execute the following statement:

```
ON ERROR GOTO 0
```

Subsequent errors print an error message and halt execution.

An ON ERROR GOTO 0 statement in an error-trapping subroutine causes GW-BASIC to stop and print the error message for the error that caused the trap. It is recommended that all error-trapping subroutines execute an ON ERROR GOTO 0 if an error is encountered for which there is no recovery action.

If an error occurs during execution of an error-handling subroutine, the GW-BASIC error message is printed and execution terminated. Error trapping does not occur within the error-handling subroutine.

Examples:

```
10 ON ERROR GOTO 1000
  .
  .
  .
1000 A=ERR:B=ERL
1010 PRINT A,B
1020 RESUME NEXT
```

Line 1010 prints the type and location of the error on the screen (see the ERR and ERL variables).

Line 1020 causes program execution to continue with the line following the error.

ON ... GOSUB and ON ... GOTO Statements

Purpose:

To branch to one of several specified line numbers, depending on the value returned when an expression is evaluated.

Syntax:

ON *expression* **GOTO** *line numbers*
ON *expression* **GOSUB** *line numbers*

Comments:

In the ON ... GOTO statement, the value of *expression* determines which line number in the list will be used for branching. For example, if the value is 3, the third line number in the list will be the destination of the branch. If the value is a noninteger, the fractional portion is rounded.

In the ON ... GOSUB statement, each line number in the list must be the first line number of a subroutine.

If the value of *expression* is zero or greater than the number of items in the list (but less than or equal to 255), GW-BASIC continues with the next executable statement.

If the value of *expression* is negative, or greater than 255, an "Illegal function call" error occurs.

Examples:

```
100 IF R<1 or R>4 then print "ERROR":END
```

If the integer value of R is less than 1, or greater than 4, program execution ends.

```
200 ON R GOTO 150,300,320,390
```

If R = 1, the program goes to line 150.

If R = 2, the program branches to line 300 and continues from there. If R = 3, the branch will be to line 320, and so on.

OPEN Statement

Purpose:

To establish input/output (I/O) to a file or device.

Syntax:

OPEN *mode,[#]file number,filename[,reclen]*

OPEN *filename* [**FOR** *mode*][**ACCESS** *access*][*lock*] **AS** [**#**]*file number* [**LEN** = *reclen*]

Comments:

filename is the name of the file.

mode (first syntax) is a string expression with one of the following characters:

Expression	Specifies
O	Sequential output mode
I	Sequential input mode
R	Random input/output mode
A	Position to end of file

mode (second syntax) determines the initial positioning within the file, and the action to be taken if the file does not exist. If the FOR mode clause is omitted, the initial position is at the beginning of the file. If the file is not found, one is created. This is the random I/O mode. That is, records may be read or written at any position within the file. The valid modes and actions taken are as follows:

INPUT   Position to the beginning of the file. A "File not found" error is given if the file does not exist.

OUTPUT   Position to the beginning of the file. If the file does not exist, one is created.

APPEND   Position to the end of the file. If the file does not exist, one is created.

RANDOM   Specifies random input or output mode.

mode must be a string constant. Do not enclose *mode* in double quotation marks. *access* can be one of the following:

READ

WRITE

READ WRITE

file number is a number between 1 and the maximum number of files allowed. The number associates an I/O buffer with a disk file or device. This association exists until a CLOSE or CLOSE file number statement is executed.

reclen is an integer expression within the range of 1–32767 that sets the record length to be used for random files. If omitted, the record length defaults to 128-byte records.

When *reclen* is used for sequential files, the default is 128 bytes, and *reclen* cannot exceed the value specified by the /**s** switch.

A disk file must be opened before any disk I/O operation can be performed on that file. OPEN allocates a buffer for I/O to the file and determines the mode of access that is used with the buffer.

More than one file can be opened for input or random access at one time with different file numbers. For example, the following statements are allowed:

```
OPEN "B:TEMP" FOR INPUT AS #1
OPEN "B:TEMP" FOR INPUT AS #2
```

However, a file may be opened only once for output or appending. For example, the following statements are illegal:

```
OPEN "TEMP" FOR OUTPUT AS #1
OPEN "TEMP" FOR OUTPUT AS #2
```

Note

Be sure to close all files before removing diskettes from the disk drives (see CLOSE and RESET).

A device may be one of the following:

A:,B:,C:...	Disk Drive
KYBD:	Keyboard (input only)
SCRN:	Screen (output only)
LPT1:	Line Printer 1
LPT2:	Line Printer 2
LPT3:	Line Printer 3
COM1:	RS-232 Communications 1
COM2:	RS-232 Communications 2

For each device, the following OPEN modes are allowed:

KYBD:	Input Only
SCRN:	Output Only
LPT1:	Output Only
LPT2:	Output Only
LPT3:	Output Only
COM1:	Input, Output, or Random Only
COM2:	Input, Output, or Random Only

Disk files allow all modes.

When a disk file is opened for APPEND, the position is initially at the end of the file, and the record number is set to the last record of the file (LOF(x)/128). PRINT, WRITE, or PUT then extends the file. The program may position elsewhere in the file with a GET statement. If this is done, the mode is changed to random and the position moves to the record indicated.

Once the position is moved from the end of the file, additional records may be appended to the file by executing a GET #x, LOF(x)/*reclen* statement. This positions the file pointer at the end of the file in preparation for appending.

Any values entered outside of the ranges given result in "Illegal function call" errors. The files are not opened.

If the file is opened as INPUT, attempts to write to the file result in "Bad file mode" errors.

If the file is opened as OUTPUT, attempts to read the file result in "Bad file mode" errors.

Opening a file for OUTPUT or APPEND fails if the file is already open in any mode.

Since it is possible to reference the same file in a subdirectory via different paths, it is nearly impossible for GW-BASIC to know that it is the same file simply by looking at the path. For this reason, GW-BASIC does not let you open the file for OUTPUT or APPEND if it is on the same disk, even if the path is different. For example if *mary* is your working directory, the following statements all refer to the same file:

```
OPEN "REPORT"
OPEN "\SALES\MARY\REPORT"
OPEN "..\MARY\REPORT"
OPEN "..\..\MARY\REPORT"
```

At any one time, it is possible to have a particular diskette filename open under more than one file number. Each file number has a different buffer, so several records from the same file may be kept in memory for quick access. This allows different modes to be used for different purposes; or, for program clarity, different file numbers to be used for different modes of access.

If the LEN = *reclen* option is used, *reclen* may not exceed the value set by the /**s:***reclen* switch option in the command line.

In a network environment, the use of the OPEN statement is based upon two different sets of circumstances:

- Devices may be shared on a network for specific purposes only, so that OPEN statements may be restricted to specific modes among those which might be requested, such as: INPUT, OUTPUT, APPEND, and default (Random).

- Files may be restricted by the implementation of an OPEN statement that allows a process to specify locking to the successfully opened file. The locking determines a guaranteed exclusivity range on that file by the process while the OPEN statement is in effect.

lock can be one of the following:

SHARED
"deny none" mode. No restrictions are placed on the read/write accessibility of the file to another process, except that the default mode is not allowed by any of the modes including SHARED.

LOCK READ
"deny read" mode. Once a file is opened with the LOCK READ access, no other process is granted read-access to that file. An attempt to open a file with this access will be unsuccessful if the file is currently open in default mode or with a read access.

LOCK WRITE
"deny write" mode. A file successfully opened with LOCK WRITE access may not be opened for a write access by another process. An attempt to open a file with this access will be unsuccessful if the file has been opened in default mode, or with a write access by another process.

LOCK READ WRITE
"deny all" or "exclusive" mode. If a file is successfully opened with this access, the process has exclusive access to the file. A file that is currently open in this mode cannot be opened again in any mode by any process.

default
"compatibility" mode, in which the compatibility with other BASICs is understood. No access is specified. The file may be opened any number of times by a process, provided that the file is not currently opened by another process. Other processes are denied access to the file while it is open under default access. Therefore, it is functionally exclusive.

When an attempt is made to open a file that has been previously accessed by another process, the error "Permission Denied" will result. An example of a situation generating this error is when a process attempts to OPEN SHARED on a file that is already OPEN LOCK READ WRITE by another process.

If an OPEN statement fails because the mode is incompatible with network-installed sharing access to a device, the error generated is "Path/File Access Error." An example of this is when a process is attempting to OPEN a file for output on a directory that has been shared for read only.

For more information about using files in a networking environment, see the LOCK and UNLOCK statements.

Examples:

```
10 OPEN "I",2,"INVEN"
```

Opens file 2, *inven*, for sequential input.

OPEN "COM(n) Statement

Purpose:

To allocate a buffer to support RS-232 asynchronous communications with other computers and peripheral devices in the same manner as OPEN for disk files.

Syntax:

OPEN "COM[*n*]:[*speed*][,*parity*][,*data*] [,*stop*][,RS][,CS[*n*]][,DS[*n*]] [,CD[*n*]][,LF] [,PE]**" AS** [**#**]*filenum* [LEN = *number*]

Comments:

COM[*n*] is a valid communications device: **com1:** or **com2:**.

speed is a literal integer specifying the transmit/receive baud rate.

Valid speeds are as follows:

75, 110, 150, 300, 600, 1200, 1800, 2400, 4800, and 9600. The default is 300 bps.

parity is a one-character literal specifying the parity for transmitting and receiving.

Valid characters specifying parity are as follows:

S	SPACE. Parity bit always transmitted and received as space (0 bit).
M	MARK. Parity bit always transmitted and received as mark (1 bit).
O	ODD. Odd transmit parity; odd receive parity checking. Default is even.
E	EVEN. Even transmit parity; even receive parity checking. Even is default.
N	NONE. No transmit parity; no receive parity checking.

data is a literal integer indicating the number of transmit/receive data bits.

Valid values for the number of data bits are 4, 5, 6, 7, and 8, the default is 7 bits.

Note

Four data bits with no parity is illegal; eight data bits with any parity is illegal.

---

stop is a literal integer expression returning a valid file number.

Valid values for number of stop bits are 1 and 2. If omitted, 75 and 110 bps transmit two stop bits. All others transmit one stop bit.

filenum is a number between 1 and the maximum number of files allowed. A communications device may be opened to only one file number at a time.

The *filenum* is associated with the file for as long as the file is open, and is used to refer other COM I/O statements to the file.

Any coding errors within the filename string result in "Bad file name" errors. An indication as to which parameters are in error is not given.

number is the maximum number of bytes that can be read from the communications buffer when using the GET or PUT default of 128 bytes.

A "Device timeout" error occurs if "data set ready" (DSR) is not detected.

The RS, CS, DS, DC, LF, and PE options affect the line signals as follows:

Option	Function
RS	suppresses RTS (request to send)
CS[*n*]	controls CTS (clear to send)
DS[*n*]	controls DSR (data set ready)
CD[*n*]	controls CD (carrier detect)
LF	sends a line feed at each return
PE	enables parity checking

n is the number of milliseconds to wait (0–65535) for that signal before a device timeout error occurs. Defaults are: CS1000, DS1000, and CD0. If RS was specified, then CS0 is the default. If *n* is omitted, then timeout is set to 0.

See Appendix F for more information about communications.

Examples:

In the following, File 1 is opened for communications with all defaults: speed at 300 bps, even parity, seven data bits, and one stop bit.

```
10 OPEN "COM1:" AS 1
```

In the following, File 2 is opened for communications at 2400 bps. Parity and number of data bits are defaulted.

```
20 OPEN "COM1:2400" AS #2
```

In the following, File 1 is opened for asynchronous I/O at 1200 bits/second. No parity is to be produced or checked.

```
10 OPEN "COM1:1200,N,8" AS #1
```

OPTION BASE Statement

Purpose:

To declare the minimum value for array subscripts.

Syntax:

OPTION BASE *n*

Comments:

n is 1 or 0. The default base is 0.

If the statement OPTION BASE 1 is executed, the lowest value an array subscript can have is 1.

An array subscript may never have a negative value.

OPTION BASE gives an error only if you change the base value. This allows chained programs to have OPTION BASE statements as long as the value is not changed from the initial setting.

Note

You must code the OPTION BASE statement before you can define or use any arrays. If an attempt is made to change the option base value after any arrays are in use, an error results.

OUT Statement

Purpose:

To send a byte to a machine output port.

Syntax:

OUT *h,j*

Comments:

h and *j* are integer expressions. *h* may be within the range of 0 to 65535. *j* may be within the range of 0 to 255. *h* is a machine port number, and *j* is the data to be transmitted.

OUT is the complementary statement to the INP function.

Examples:

```
100 OUT 12345,225
```

Outputs the decimal value 225 to port number 12345. In assembly language, this is equivalent to the following:

```
MOV DX,12345
MOV AL,255
OUT DX,AL
```

PAINT Statement

Purpose:

To fill in a graphics figure with the selected attribute.

Syntax:

PAINT (*x start,y start*)[*,paint attribute*[*,border attribute*][*,bckgrnd attribute*]]

Comments:

The PAINT statement fills in an arbitrary graphics figure of the specified border attribute with the specified paint attribute. If *paint attribute* is not given, it will default to the foreground attribute (3 or 1). *border attribute* defaults to *paint attribute*. See the COLOR and PALETTE statements for more information.

PAINT must start on a nonborder point; otherwise, PAINT will have no effect.

PAINT can fill any figure, but painting jagged edges or very complex figures may result in an "Out of memory" error. The CLEAR statement may be used to increase the amount of stack space available.

Points that are specified outside the limits of the screen will not be plotted and no error will occur.

See the SCREEN statement for a description of the different screen modes.

Paint Tiling

PAINT tiling is similar to LINE styling. Like LINE, PAINT looks at a tiling mask each time a point is put down on the screen.

If *paint attribute* is omitted, the standard foreground attribute is used.

If *paint attribute* is a numeric formula, then the number must be a valid color, and it is used to paint the area as before.

If *paint attribute* is a string formula, then tiling is performed as follows:

The tile mask is always eight bits wide and may be from 1 to 64 bytes long. Each byte in the tile string masks eight bits along the x axis when putting down points. Each byte of the tile string is rotated as required to align along the y axis, such that:

tile_byte_mask = y MOD tile_length

where *y* is the position of the graphics cursor on the y axis.

tile_length is the length in bytes of the tile string defined by the user (1 to 64 bytes).

This is done so that the tile pattern is replicated uniformly over the entire screen (as if a PAINT (0,0).. were used).

```
x Increases --> Bit of Tile Byte
x,y       8 7 6 5 4 3 2 1

0,0       !x!x!x!x!x!x!x!x!    Tile byte 1
0,1       !x!x!x!x!x!x!x!x!    Tile byte 2
0,2       !x!x!x!x!x!x!x!x!    Tile byte 3
  .
  .
  .
0,63      !x!x!x!x!x!x!x!x!    Tile byte 64
                              (maximum allowed)
```

In high-resolution mode (SCREEN 2), the screen can be painted with Xs by the following statement:

```
PAINT (320,100),CHR$(&H81)+CHR$(&H42)+CHR$(&H24)+
CHR$(&H18)+CHR$(&H18)+CHR$(&H24)+CHR$(&H81)
```

This appears on the screen as follows:

```
x increases -->

0,0    !x! ! ! ! ! ! !x!    CHR$(&H81)    Tile byte 1
0,1    ! !x! ! ! ! !x! !    CHR$(&H42)    Tile byte 2
0,2    ! ! !x! ! !x! ! !    CHR$(&H24)    Tile byte 3
0,3    ! ! ! !x!x! ! ! !    CHR$(&H18)    Tile byte 4
0,4    ! ! ! !x!x! ! ! !    CHR$(&H18)    Tile byte 5
0,5    ! ! !x! ! !x! ! !    CHR$(&H24)    Tile byte 6
0,6    ! !x! ! ! ! !x! !    CHR$(&H42)    Tile byte 7
0,7    !x! ! ! ! ! ! !x!    CHR$(&H81)    Tile byte 8
```

Since there are two bits per pixel in medium-resolution mode (SCREEN 1), each byte of the tile pattern describes only four pixels. In this case, every two bits of the tile byte describes one of the four possible colors associated with each of the four pixels to be put down.

bckgrnd attribute specifies the background tile pattern or color byte to skip when checking for boundary termination. *bckgrnd attribute* is a string formula returning one character. When omitted, the default is CHR$(0).

Occasionally, you may want to paint tile over an already painted area that is the same color as two consecutive lines in the tile pattern. PAINT quits when it encounters two consecutive lines of the same color as the point being set (the point is surrounded). It is not possible to draw alternating blue and red lines on a red background without *bckgrnd attribute*. PAINT stops as soon as the first red pixel is drawn. By specifying red (CHR$(&HAA)) as the background attribute, the red line is drawn over the red background.

You cannot specify more than two consecutive bytes in the tile string that match the background attribute. Specifying more than two results in an "Illegal function call" error.

Examples:

```
10 CLS
20 SCREEN 1
30 LINE (0,0)-(100,150),2,B
40 PAINT (50,50),1,2
50 LOCATE 20,1
```

The PAINT statement in line 40 fills in the box drawn in line 30 with color 1.

PALETTE, PALETTE USING Statements

Purpose:

Changes one or more of the colors in the palette

Syntax:

PALETTE [*attribute,color*]
PALETTE USING *integer-array-name* (*arrayindex*)

Comments:

The PALETTE statement works *only* for systems equipped with the IBM®
Enhanced Graphics Adapter (EGA). A GW-BASIC palette contains a set of
colors, with each color specified by an *attribute*. Each *attribute* is paired
with an actual display *color*. This *color* determines the actual visual color
on the screen, and is dependent on the setting of your screen mode and your
actual physical hardware display.

PALETTE with no arguments sets the palette to a known initial setting.
This setting is the same as the setting when colors are first initialized.

If arguments are specified, *color* will be displayed whenever *attribute* is
specified in any statement that specifies a color. Any color changes on the
screen occur immediately. Note that when graphics statements use color
arguments, they are actually referring to attributes and not actual colors.
PALETTE pairs attributes with actual colors.

For example, assume that the current palette consists of *colors* 0, 1, 2,
and 3. The following DRAW statement:

```
DRAW "C3L100"
```

selects attribute 3, and draws a line of 100 pixels using the color associated
with the attribute 3, in this case, also 3. If the following statement:

```
PALETTE 3,2
```

is executed, then the color associated with attribute 3 is changed to color 2.
All text or graphics currently displayed on the screen using attribute 3 are
instantaneously changed to color 2. All text or graphics subsequently displayed with attribute 3 will also be displayed in color 2. The new palette of
colors will contain 0, 1, 2, and 2.

231

With the USING option, all entries in the palette can be modified in one PALETTE statement. The *integer-array-name* argument is the name of an integer array, and the *arrayindex* specifies the index of the first array element in the *integer-array-name* to use in setting your palette. Each *attribute* in the palette is assigned a corresponding *color* from this integer array. The array must be dimensioned large enough to set all the palette entries after *arrayindex*. For example, if you are assigning colors to all 16 attributes, and the index of the first array element given in your PALETTE USING statement is 5, then the array must be dimensioned to hold at least 20 elements (since the number of elements from $5 - 20$, inclusive, is 16):

```
DIM PAL%(20)
   .
   .
   .
PALETTE USING PAL%(5)
```

If the *color* argument in an array entry is -1, then the mapping for the associated *attribute* is not changed. All other negative numbers are illegal values for *color*.

You can use the color argument in the COLOR statement to set the default text color. (Remember that color arguments in other BASIC statements are actually what are called *attributes* in this discussion.) This color argument specifies the way that text characters appear on the display screen. Under a common initial palette setting, points colored with the *attribute* 0 appear as black on the display screen. Using the PALETTE statement, you could, for example, change the mapping of *attribute* 0 from black to white.

Remember that a PALETTE statement executed without any parameters assigns all *attributes* their default *colors*.

The following table lists *attribute* and *color* ranges for various monitor types and screen modes:

Table 1
SCREEN Color and Attribute Ranges

SCREEN Mode	Monitor Attached	Adapter	Attribute Range	Color Range
0	Monochrome	MDPA	NA	NA
	Monochrome	EGA	$0-15$	$0-2$
	Color	CGA	NA	$0-31$[a]
	Color/Enhanced[d]	EGA	$0-31$[a]	$0-15$
1	Color	CGA	NA	$0-3$
	Color/Enhanced[d]	EGA	$0-3$	$0-15$
2	Color	CGA	NA	$0-1$
	Color/Enhanced[d]	EGA	$0-1$	$0-15$
7	Color/Enhanced[d]	EGA	$0-15$	$0-15$
8	Color/Enhanced[d]	EGA	$0-15$	$0-15$
9	Enhanced[d]	EGA[b]	$0-3$	$0-15$
	Enhanced[d]	EGA[c]	$0-15$	$0-63$
10	Monochrome	EGA	$0-3$	$0-8$

[a] Attributes $16-31$ refer to blinking versions of colors $0-15$
[b] With 64K of EGA memory
[c] With greater than 64K of EGA memory
[d] IBM Enhanced Color Display
NA = Not Applicable
CGA = IBM Color Graphics Adapter
EGA = IBM Enhanced Graphics Adapter
MDPA = IBM Monochrome Display and Printer Adapter

See the SCREEN statement reference page for the list of colors available for various SCREEN mode, monitor, and graphics adapter combinations.

Examples:

```
PALETTE 0,2      'Changes all points colored with attribute 0
                 'to color 2

PALETTE 0,-1     'Does not modify the palette

PALETTE USING A%(0)      'Changes each palette entry. Since the
                         'array is initialized to zero when it
                         'is first declared, all attributes are
                         'now mapped to display color zero. The
                         'screen will now appear as one single
                         'color. However, it will still be
                         'possible to execute BASIC statements.

PALETTE          'Sets each palette entry to its appropriate
                 'initial display color. Actual initial colors
                 'depend on your screen hardware configuration.
```

PCOPY Command

Purpose:

To copy one screen page to another in all screen modes.

Syntax:

PCOPY *sourcepage*, *destinationpage*

Comments:

The *sourcepage* is an integer expression in the range 0 to *n*, where *n* is determined by the current video-memory size and the size per page for the current screen mode.

The *destinationpage* has the same requirements as the *sourcepage*.

For more information, see CLEAR and SCREEN.

Examples:

This copies the contents of page 1 to page 2:

```
PCOPY 1,2
```

PEEK Function

Purpose:

To read from a specified memory location.

Syntax:

PEEK(*a*)

Comments:

Returns the byte (decimal integer within the range of 0 to 255) read from the specified memory location *a*. *a* must be within the range of 0 to 65535.

The DEF SEG statement last executed determines the absolute address that will be peeked into.

PEEK is the complementary function to the POKE statement.

Examples:

```
10 A=PEEK(&H5A00)
```

The value of the byte, stored in user-assigned hex offset memory location 5A00 (23040 decimal), will be stored in the variable A.

PEN Statement and Function

Purpose:

To read the light pen.

Syntax:

As a statement:

PEN ON
PEN OFF
PEN STOP

As a function:

$x = P(n)$

Comments:

x is the numeric variable receiving the PEN value.

n is an integer within the range of 0 to 9.

PEN ON enables the PEN read function.

PEN OFF disables the PEN read function.

PEN STOP disables trapping. It remembers the event so that immediate trapping occurs when PEN ON is executed.

$x = PEN(n)$ reads the light pen coordinates.

The PEN function is initially off. A PEN ON statement must be executed before any PEN read function calls can be made, or a PEN read function call results in an "Illegal function call" error.

Light pen coordinates:

$n = 0$	If PEN was down since last poll, returns -1; if not, returns 0.

$n = 1$	Returns the x-pixel coordinate when PEN was last activated. The range is within 0 to 319 for medium resolution, 0 to 639 for high resolution.
$n = 2$	Returns the y-pixel coordinate when PEN was last activated. The range is within 0 to 199.
$n = 3$	Returns the current PEN switch value. Returns -1 if down, 0 if up.
$n = 4$	Returns the last known valid x-pixel coordinate. The range is within 0 to 319 for medium resolution, or 0 to 639 for high resolution.
$n = 5$	Returns the last known valid y-pixel coordinate. The range is within 0 to 199.
$n = 6$	Returns the character row position when PEN was last activated. The range is within 1 to 24.
$n = 7$	Returns the character column position when PEN was last activated. The range is within 1 to 40, or 1 to 80, depending on the screen width.
$n = 8$	Returns the last known valid character row. The range is within 1 to 24.
$n = 9$	Returns the last known valid character column position. The range is within 1 to 40, or 1 to 80, depending on the screen width.

For execution speed improvements, turn the pen off with a PEN OFF statement for those programs not using the light pen.

When the pen is in the border area of the screen, the values returned will be inaccurate.

Examples:

```
50 PEN ON
60 FOR I=1 to 500
70 X=PEN(0):X1=PEN(3)
80 Print X,X1
90 NEXT
100 PEN OFF
```

This example prints the pen value since the last poll and the current value.

PLAY Statement

Purpose:

To play music by embedding a music macro language into the string data type.

Syntax:

PLAY *string expression*

Comments:

The single-character commands in PLAY are as follows:

A-G [#, +, -]   A-G are notes. # or + following a note produces a sharp; - produces a flat.

     Any note followed by #, +, or - must refer to a black key on a piano.

L(*n*)   Sets the length of each note. L4 is a quarter note, L1 is a whole note, and so on. *n* may be from 1 to 64.

     Length may also follow the note to change the length for that note only. A16 is equivalent to L16A.

MF   Music foreground. PLAY and SOUND statements are to run in foreground. That is, each subsequent note or sound is not started until the previous note or sound is finished. This is the initial default.

MB   Music background. PLAY and SOUND statements are to run in background. That is, each note or sound is placed in a buffer allowing the BASIC program to continue execution while music plays in the background. As many as 32 notes (or rests) can be played in background at one time.

MN	Music normal. Each note plays seven-eighths of the time determined by L (length).
ML	Music legato. Each note plays the full period set by L.
MS	Music staccato. Each note plays three-quarters of the time determined by L.
N(*n*)	Play note *n*. *n* may range from 0 to 84. In the 7 possible octaves, there are 84 notes. *n* set to 0 indicates a rest.
O(*n*)	Octave 0 sets the current octave. There are 7 octaves (0 through 6). Default is 4. Middle C is at the beginning of octave 3.
P(*n*)	Pause. P may range from 1–64.
T(*n*)	Tempo. T sets the number of L4s in a minute. *n* may range from 32–255. Default is 120.
. (period)	A period after a note increases the playing time of the note by 3/2 times the period determined by L (length of the note) times T (tempo). Multiple periods can appear after a note, and the playing time is scaled accordingly. For example, A. will cause the note A to play one and one half times the playing time determined by L (length of the note) times T (the tempo); two periods placed after A (A..) will cause the note to be played at 9/4 times its ascribed value; an A with three periods (A...) at 27/8, etc.
	Periods may also appear after a P (pause), and increase the pause length as described above.
X*string*;	Executes a substring, where *string* is a variable assigned to a string of PLAY commands.
	Because of the slow clock interrupt rate, some notes do not play at higher tempos; for example, 1.64 at T255. These note/tempo combinations must be determined through experimentation.

>*n*	A greater-than symbol preceding the note *n* plays the note in the next higher octave.
<*n*	A less-than symbol preceding the note *n* plays the note in the next lower octave.

Note

Numeric arguments follow the same syntax described under the DRAW statement.

---

n as an argument can be a constant, or it can be a variable with = in front of it (= *variable*). A semicolon is required after the variable and also after the variable in X*string*.

PLAY(n) Function

Purpose:

To return the number of notes currently in the background music queue.

Syntax:

PLAY(*n*)

Comments:

n is a dummy argument, and may be any value.

PLAY(*n*) returns 0 when in music foreground mode.

The maximum returned value of x is 32.

Examples:

```
10 ' when 4 notes are left in
20 ' queue play another tune
30 PLAY "MBABCDABCDABCD"
40 IF PLAY (0) =4 then 200
.
.
.
200 PLAY "MBCDEFCDEF"
```

PMAP Function (Graphics)

Purpose:

To map expressions to logical or physical coordinates.

Syntax:

$x = $ **PMAP** (*exp,function*)

Comments:

This function is valid for graphics modes only.

x is the physical coordinate of the point that is to be mapped.

exp is a numeric variable or expression.

Function	Maps
0	logical expressions to physical x
1	logical expressions to physical y
2	physical expressions to logical x
3	physical expressions to logical y

PMAP is used with WINDOW and VIEW to translate coordinates.

POINT Function

Purpose:

To read the color or attribute value of a pixel from the screen.

Syntax:

POINT(*x,y*)
POINT(*function*)

Comments:

In the first syntax, *x* and *y* are coordinates of the point to be examined.

If the point given is out of range, the value -1 is returned.

See the COLOR and PALETTE statements for valid color and attribute values.

POINT with one argument allows you to retrieve the current graphics coordinates.

POINT(*function*) returns the value of the current x or y graphics coordinates as follows:

Function	Returns
0	the current physical x coordinate.
1	the current physical y coordinate.
2	the current logical x coordinate if WINDOW is active; otherwise, it returns the current physical x coordinate as in 0 above.
3	the current logical y coordinate if WINDOW is active; otherwise, it returns the current physical y coordinate as in 1 above.

Example 1:

```
10 SCREEN 1
20 FOR C=0 TO 3
30 PSET (10,10),C
40 IF POINT(10,10)<>C THEN PRINT "BROKEN BASIC="
50 NEXT C
RUN
```

Example 2:

The following inverts the current state of a point:

```
10 SCREEN 2
20 IF POINT(I,I)<>0 THEN PRESET(I,I) ELSE PSET(I,I)
RUN
```

Example 3:

The following is another way to invert a point:

```
20 PSET (I,I),1-POINT(I,I)
RUN
```

POKE Statement

Purpose:

To write (poke) a byte of data into a memory location.

Syntax:

POKE *a,b*

Comments:

a and *b* are integer expressions.

The integer expression *a* is the offset address of the memory location to be poked. The DEF SEG statement last executed determines the address. GW-BASIC does not check any offsets that are specified.

The integer expression *b* is the data to be poked.

b must be within the range of 0 to 255. *a* must be within the range of 0 to 65535.

The complementary function to POKE is PEEK. The argument to PEEK is an address from which a byte is to be read.

POKE and PEEK are useful for efficient data storage, for loading assembly language subroutines, and for passing arguments and results to and from assembly language subroutines.

Examples:

```
20 POKE &H5A00,&HFF
```

Places the decimal value 255 (&HFF) into the hex offset location (23040 decimal). See the PEEK function example.

POS Function

Purpose:

To return the current cursor position.

Syntax:

POS(c)

Comments:

The leftmost position is 1.

c is a dummy argument.

Examples:

```
10 CLS
20 WIDTH 80
30 A$=INKEY$:IF A$=""THEN GOTO 30 ELSE PRINT A$;
40 IF POS(X)>10 THEN PRINT CHR$(13);
50 GOTO 30
```

Causes a carriage return after the 10th character is printed on each line of the screen.

PRESET and PSET Statements

Purpose:

To display a point at a specified place on the screen during use of the graphics mode.

Syntax:

PRESET(*x,y*)[*,color*]
PSET(*x,y*)[*,color*]

Comments:

(*x,y*) represents the coordinates of the point.

color is the color of the point.

Coordinates can be given in either absolute or relative form.

Absolute Form

(*absolute x,absolute y*) is more common and refers directly to a point without regard to the last point referenced. For example:

```
(10,10)
```

Relative Form

STEP (*x offset,y offset*) is a point relative to the most recent point referenced. For example:

```
STEP(10,10)
```

Coordinate values can be beyond the edge of the screen. However, values outside the integer range (−32768 to 32767) cause an "Overflow" error.

(0,0) is always the upper-left corner and (0,199) is the lower-left corner in both high resolution and medium resolution.

See the COLOR and PALETTE statements for more information.

If the value for color is greater than 3, an "Illegal function call" error is returned.

Example 1:

The following draws a diagonal line from (0,0) to (100,100).

```
10 CLS
20 SCREEN 1
30 FOR I=0 TO 100
40 PSET (I,I)
50 NEXT
60 LOCATE 14,1
```

Example 2:

The following clears out the line by setting each pixel to 0.

```
40 FOR I=100 TO 0 STEP -1
50 PSET(I,I),0
60 NEXT I
```

PRINT Statement

Purpose:

To output a display to the screen.

Syntax:

PRINT [*list of expressions*][;]
?[*list of expressions*][;]

Comments:

If *list of expressions* is omitted, a blank line is displayed.

If *list of expressions* is included, the values of the expressions are displayed. Expressions in the list may be numeric and/or string expressions, separated by commas, spaces, or semicolons. String constants in the list must be enclosed in double quotation marks.

For more information about strings, see the STRING$ function.

A question mark (?) may be used in place of the word PRINT when using the GW-BASIC program editor.

Print Positions

GW-BASIC divides the line into print zones of 14 spaces. The position of each item printed is determined by the punctuation used to separate the items in the list:

Separator	Print Position
,	Beginning of next zone
;	Immediately after last value
space(s)	Immediately after last value

If a comma, semicolon, or SPC or TAB function ends an expression list, the next PRINT statement begins printing on the same line, accordingly spaced. If the expression list ends without a comma, semicolon, or SPC or TAB function, a carriage return is placed at the end of the lines (GW-BASIC places the cursor at the beginning of the next line).

A carriage return/line feed is automatically inserted after printing width characters, where the width is 40 or 80, as defined in the WIDTH statement. This results in two lines being skipped when you print exactly 40 (or 80) characters, unless the PRINT statement ends in a semicolon.

When numbers are printed on the screen, the numbers are always followed by a space. Positive numbers are preceded by a space. Negative numbers are preceded by a minus (−) sign. Single-precision numbers are represented with seven or fewer digits in a fixed-point or integer format.

See the LPRINT and LPRINT USING statements for information on sending data to be printed on a printer.

Examples:

```
10 X$= STRING$(10,45)
20 PRINT X$"MONTHLY REPORT" X$
----------MONTHLY REPORT----------
Ok
```

45 is the decimal equivalent of the ASCII symbol for the minus (−) sign.

PRINT USING Statement

Purpose:

To print strings or numbers using a specified format.

Syntax:

PRINT USING *string expressions;list of expressions*[;]

Comments:

string expressions is a string literal or variable consisting of special formatting characters. The formatting characters determine the field and the format of printed strings or numbers.

list of expressions consists of the string or numeric expressions separated by semicolons.

String Fields

The following three characters may be used to format the string field:

!	Specifies that only the first character in the string is to be printed.
\n spaces\	Specifies that $2+n$ characters from the string are to be printed.
	If the backslashes are typed with no spaces, two characters are printed; if the backslashes are typed with one space, three characters are printed, and so on.
	If the string is longer than the field, the extra characters are ignored. If the field is longer than the string, the string is left-justified in the field and padded with spaces on the right. For example:

```
10 A$="LOOK":B$="OUT"
30 PRINT USING "!";A$;B$
40 PRINT USING"\  \";A$;B$
50 PRINT USING"\    \";A$;B$;"!!"
RUN
```

```
RUN
LO
LOOKOUT
LOOK OUT!!
```

    &   Specifies a variable length string field. When the field is specified with &, the string is output exactly as input. For example:

```
10 A$="LOOK":B$="OUT"
20 PRINT USING "!";A$
30 PRINT USING "&";B$
RUN
LOUT
```

Numeric Fields

The following special characters may be used to format the numeric field:

    #   A pound sign is used to represent each digit position. Digit positions are always filled. If the number to be printed has fewer digits than positions specified, the number is right-justified (preceded by spaces) in the field.

A decimal point may be inserted at any position in the field. If the format string specifies that a digit is to precede the decimal point, the digit always is printed (as 0 if necessary). Numbers are rounded as necessary. For example:

```
PRINT USING "##.##";.78
0.78
OK

PRINT USING "###.##";987.654
987.65
OK

PRINT USING "##.##"   ;10.2,5.3,66.789,.234
10.20    5.30    66.79    0.23
```

In the last example, three spaces were inserted at the end of the format string to separate the printed values on the line.

+   A plus sign at the beginning or end of the format string causes the sign of the number (plus or minus) to be printed before or after the number.

−   A minus sign at the end of the format field causes negative numbers to be printed with a trailing minus sign. For example:

```
PRINT USING"+##.##";-68.95,2.4,55.6,-9
-68.95 +2.40 +55.60 -0.90
OK

PRINT USING"##.##-";-68.95,22.449,-7.01
68.95  22.45  7.01-
OK
```

**   A double asterisk at the beginning of the format string causes leading spaces in the numeric field to be filled with asterisks. The ** also specifies two more digit positions. For example:

```
PRINT USING "**#.#";12.39,-0.9,765.1
*12.4*  -09765.1
Ok
```

$$ A double dollar sign at the beginning of the format string causes a dollar sign to be printed to the immediate left of the formatted number. The $$ specifies two more digit positions, one of which is the dollar sign. The exponential format cannot be used with $$. Negative numbers cannot be used unless the minus sign trails to the right. For example:

```
PRINT USING "$$###.##";456.78
$456.78
Ok
```

**$ The **$ at the beginning of the format string combines the effects of the above two symbols. Leading spaces are filled with asterisks, and a dollar sign is printed before the number. **$ specifies three more digit positions, one of which is the dollar sign. For example:

```
PRINT USING "**$##.##";2.34
***$2.34
```

, A comma to the left of the decimal point in the format string causes a comma to be printed to the left of every third digit to the left of the decimal point. A comma at the end of the format string is printed as part of the string.

```
PRINT USING "####.##";1234.5
1234.50
Ok
```

^^^^ Four carets may be placed after the digit position characters to specify exponential format. The four carets allow space for E + xx to be printed. Any decimal point position may be specified. The significant digits are left-justified, and the exponent is adjusted. Unless a leading + or trailing + or − is specified, one digit position is used to the left of the decimal point to print a space or a minus sign. For example:

```
PRINT USING "##.##^^^^";234.56
2.35E+02
Ok
```

```
PRINT USING ".####^^^^-";888888
Ok
```

```
PRINT USING "+.##^^^^";123
+.12E+03
Ok
```

Note that in the above examples the comma is *not* used as a delimiter with the exponential format.

_ An underscore in the format string causes the next character to be output as a literal character. For example:

```
PRINT USING "_!##.##_!";12.34
!12.34!
Ok
```

The literal character itself may be an underscore by placing "_" in the format string.

%   A percent sign is printed in front of the number if the number to be printed is larger than the specified numeric field. If rounding causes the number to exceed the field, a percent sign is printed in front of the rounded number. For example:

```
PRINT USING "##.##";111.22
%111.22

PRINT USING ".##"';.999
%1.00
```

If the number of digits specified exceeds 24, an "Illegal function call" error results.

PRINT# and PRINT# USING Statements

Purpose:

To write data to a sequential disk file.

Syntax:

PRINT#*file number,***[USING***string expressions;***]***list of expressions*

Comments:

file number is the number used when the file was opened for output.

string expressions consists of the formatting characters described in the PRINT USING statement.

list of expressions consists of the numeric and/or string expressions to be written to the file.

Double quotation marks are used as delimiters for numeric and/or string expressions. The first double quotation mark opens the line for input; the second double quotation mark closes it.

If numeric or string expressions are to be printed as they are input, they must be surrounded by double quotation marks. If the double quotation marks are omitted, the value assigned to the numeric or string expression is printed. If no value has been assigned, 0 is assumed. The double quotation marks do not appear on the screen. For example:

```
10  PRINT#1,A
0

10  A=26
20  PRINT#1,A
26

10  A=26
20  PRINT#1,"A"
A
```

If double quotation marks are required within a string, use CHR$(34) (the ASCII character for double quotation marks). For example:

```
100 PRINT#1,"He said,"Hello", I think"
He said, 0, I think
```

because the machine assigns the value 0 the variable "Hello."

```
100 PRINT#1, "He said, "CHR$(34)
"Hello,"CHR$(34) " I think."
He said, "Hello," I think
```

If the strings contain commas, semicolons, or significant leading blanks, surround them with double quotation marks. The following example will input "CAMERA" to A$, and "AUTOMATIC 93604-1" to B$:

```
10 A$="CAMERA,AUTOMATIC":B$="93604-1"
20 PRINT#1,A$;B$
30 INPUT#1,A$,B$
```

To separate these strings properly, write successive double quotation marks using CHR$(34). For example:

```
40 PRINT#1,CHR$(34);A$;CHR$(34);CHR$(34);B$; CHR$(34)

"CAMERA,AUTOMATIC""93604-1"
```

The PRINT# statement may also be used with the USING option to control the format of the disk file. For example:

```
PRINT#1,USING"$$###.##.";J;K;L
```

PRINT# does not compress data on the diskette. An image of the data is written to the diskette, just as it would be displayed on the terminal screen with a PRINT statement. For this reason, be sure to delimit the data on the diskette so that it is input correctly from the diskette.

In *list of expressions*, numeric expressions must be delimited by semicolons. For example:

```
PRINT#1,A;B;C;X;Y;Z
```

If commas are used as delimiters, the extra blanks inserted between print fields will also be written to the diskette. Commas have no effect, however, if used with the exponential format.

String expressions must be separated by semicolons in the list. To format the string expressions correctly on the diskette, use explicit delimiters in *list of expressions.* For example, the following:

```
10 A$="CAMERA":B$="93604-1"
20 PRINT#1,A$,B$
```

gives a diskette image of:

```
CAMERA93604-1
```

Because there are no delimiters, this would not be input as two separate strings. To correct the problem, insert explicit delimiters into the PRINT# statement as follows:

```
30 PRINT#1,A$;",";B$
```

This gives the following diskette image, which can be read back into two string variables:

```
CAMERA,93604-1
```

PUT Statement (Files)

Purpose:

To write a record from a random buffer to a random disk file.

Syntax:

PUT[#]*file number*[*,record number*]

Comments:

file number is the number under which the file was opened.

record number is the number of the record. If it is omitted, the record has the next available record number (after the last PUT).

The largest possible record number is $2^{32} - 1$. This will allow you to have large files with short record lengths. The smallest possible record number is 1.

The PRINT#, PRINT# USING, LSET, RSET, or WRITE# statement may be used to put characters in the random file buffer before a PUT statement.

In the case of WRITE#, GW-BASIC pads the buffer with spaces up to an enter.

Any attempt to read or write past the end of the buffer causes a "Field overflow" error.

PUT can be used for communications files. Here *record number* is the number of bytes written to the file. *Record number* must be less than or equal to the length of the buffer set in the OPEN "COM(n) statement.

PUT Statement (Graphics)

Purpose:

To transfer graphics images to the screen.

Syntax:

PUT(*x,y*),*array*,[,*action verb*]

Comments:

action verb may be PSET, PRESET, AND, OR, or XOR.

(*x,y*) are the coordinates of the top-left corner of the image to be transferred.

The PUT and GET statements transfer graphics images to and from the screen. PUT and GET make possible animation and high-speed object motion in either graphics mode.

The PUT statement transfers the image stored in the array onto the screen. The specified point is the coordinate of the upper-left corner of the image. An "Illegal function call" error results if the image to be transferred is too large to fit onto the screen.

The action verb is used to interact the transferred image with the image already on the screen. PSET transfers the data onto the screen verbatim.

PRESET is the same as PSET except that an inverse image (black on white) is produced.

AND transfers the image only if an image already exists under the transferred image.

OR superimposes the image onto the existing image.

XOR is a special mode often used for animation. XOR causes the points on the screen to be inverted where a point exists in the array image. This behavior is exactly like the cursor on the screen.

XOR is especially useful for animation. When an image is put against a complex background twice, the background is restored unchanged. An object can be moved around the screen without obliterating the background.

The default action mode is XOR.

For more information about effects within the different modes, see the COLOR, PALETTE, and SCREEN statements.

Animation of an object is usually performed as follows:

1. Put the object(s) on the screen.

2. Recalculate the new position of the object(s).

3. Put the object(s) on the screen a second time at the old location(s) to remove the old image(s).

4. Return to Step 1, this time putting the object(s) at the new location.

Movement done this way leaves the background unchanged. Flicker can be cut down by minimizing the time between Steps 4 and 1, and by making sure that there is enough time delay between Steps 1 and 3. If more than one object is being animated, process every object at once, one step at a time.

If it is not important to preserve the background, animation can be performed using the PSET action verb.

Leave a border around the image (when it is first gotten) as large or larger than the maximum distance the object will move. Thus, when an object is moved, this border effectively erases any points. This method may be somewhat faster than the method using XOR described above since only one PUT is required to move an object. However, the image to be PUT must be larger than the existing image.

Examples:

```
10 CLS:SCREEN 1
20 PSET (130,120)
30 DRAW "U25;E7;R20;D32;L6;U12;L14"
40 DRAW "D12;L6":PSET(137,102)
50 DRAW "U4;E4;R8;D8;L12"
60 PSET (137,88)
70 DRAW "E4;R20;D32;G4":PAINT (131,119)
80 DIM A (500)
90 GET (125,130)-(170,80),A
```

```
100 FOR I= 1 TO 1000:NEXT I
110 PUT (20,20),A,PSET
120 FOR I= 1 TO 1000:NEXT i
130 GET (125,130)-(170,80),A
140 FOR I= 1 TO 1000:NEXT I
150 PUT (220,130),A,PRESET
```

RANDOMIZE Statement

Purpose:

To reseed the random number generator.

Syntax:

RANDOMIZE [*expression*]
RANDOMIZE TIMER

Comments:

If *expression* is omitted, GW-BASIC suspends program execution and asks for a value by displaying the following line:

```
Random number seed (-32768 to 32767)?
```

If the random number generator is not reseeded, the RND function returns the same sequence of random numbers each time the program is run.

To change the sequence of random numbers every time the program is run, place a RANDOMIZE statement at the beginning of the program, and change the argument with each run (see RND function).

RANDOMIZE with no arguments will prompt you for a new seed. RAN-DOMIZE [*expression*] will not force floating-point values to integer. *expression* may be any numeric formula.

To get a new random seed without prompting, use the new numeric TIMER function as follows:

```
RANDOMIZE TIMER
```

Example 1:

The internal clock can be set at intervals.

```
10 RANDOMIZE TIMER
20 FOR I=1 to 5
30 PRINT RND;
40 NEXT I
```

```
RUN
.88598    .484668    .586328    .119426    .709225
Ok

RUN
.803506    .162462    .929364    .292443    .322921
Ok
```

Example 2:

The internal clock can be used for random number seed.

```
5   N=VAL(MID$(TIME$,7,2))    'get seconds for seed
10  RANDOMIZE N               'install number
20  PRINT N                   'print seconds
30  PRINT RND                 'print random number generated
RUN
36
.2466638
Ok
RUN
 37
.6530511
Ok
RUN
 38
 5.943847E+02
Ok
RUN
  40
 .8722131
Ok
```

READ Statement

Purpose:

To read values from a DATA statement and assign them to variables.

Syntax:

READ *list of variables*

Comments:

A READ statement must always be used with a DATA statement.

READ statements assign variables to DATA statement values on a one-to-one basis.

READ statement variables may be numeric or string, and the values read must agree with the variable types specified. If they do not agree, a "Syntax" error results.

A single READ statement may access one or more DATA statements. They are accessed in order. Several READ statements may access the same DATA statement.

If the number of variables in *list of variables* exceeds the number of elements in the DATA statement(s), an "Out of data" message is printed.

If the number of variables specified is fewer than the number of elements in the DATA statement(s), subsequent READ statements begin reading data at the first unread element. If there are no subsequent READ statements, the extra data is ignored.

To reread DATA statements from the start, use the RESTORE statement.

Examples:

```
      .
      .
      .
80 FOR I=1 TO 10
90 READ A(I)
100 NEXT I
110 DATA 3.08,5.19,3.12,3.98,4.24
120 DATA 5.08,5.55,4.00,3.16,3.37
      .
      .
      .
```

This program segment reads the values from the DATA statements into array A. After execution, the value of A(1) is 3.08, and so on. The DATA statement (lines 110-120) may be placed anywhere in the program; they may even be placed ahead of the READ statement.

```
5 PRINT
10 PRINT "CITY","STATE","ZIP"
20 READ C$,S$,Z
30 DATA "DENVER,","COLORADO",80211
40 PRINT C$,S$,Z
RUN

CITY        STATE       ZIP
DENVER,COLORADO 80211
Ok
```

This program reads string and numeric data from the DATA statement in line 30.

REM Statement

Purpose:

To allow explanatory remarks to be inserted in a program.

Syntax:

REM[*comment*]
'[*comment*]

Comments:

REM statements are not executed, but are output exactly as entered when the program is listed.

Once a REM or its abbreviation, an apostrophe ('), is encountered, the program ignores everything else until the next line number or program end is encountered.

REM statements may be branched into from a GOTO or GOSUB statement, and execution continues with the first executable statement after the REM statement. However, the program runs faster if the branch is made to the first statement.

Remarks may be added to the end of a line by preceding the remark with an apostrophe (') instead of REM.

Note

Do not use REM in a DATA statement because it will be considered to be legal data.

Examples:

.
.
.
```
120  REM CALCULATE AVERAGE VELOCITY
130  FOR I=1 TO 20
440  SUM=SUM+V(I)
450  NEXT I
```
.
.
.

or

.
.
.
```
129  FOR I=1 TO 20 'CALCULATED AVERAGE VELOCITY
130  SUM=SUM+V(I)
140  NEXT I
```
.
.
.

RENUM Command

Purpose:

To renumber program lines.

Syntax:

RENUM[*new number*],[*old number*][,*increment***R**]]

Comments:

new number is the first line number to be used in the new sequence. The default is 10.

old number is the line in the current program where renumbering is to begin. The default is the first line of the program.

increment is the increment to be used in the new sequence. The default is 10.

RENUM also changes all line number references following ELSE, GOTO, GOSUB, THEN, ON...GOTO, ON...GOSUB, RESTORE, RESUME, and ERL statements to reflect the new line numbers. If a nonexistent line number appears after one of these statements, the error message "Undefined line *x* in *y*" appears. The incorrect line number reference *x* is not changed by RENUM, but line number *y* may be changed.

RENUM cannot be used to change the order of program lines (for example, RENUM 15,30 when the program has three lines numbered 10, 20 and 30) or to create line numbers greater than 65529. An "Illegal function call" error results.

Examples:

```
RENUM
```

Renumbers the entire program. The first new line number will be 10. Lines increment by 10.

```
RENUM 300,,50
```

Renumbers the entire program. The first new line number will be 300. Lines increment by 50.

```
RENUM 1000,900,20
```

Renumbers the lines from 900 up so they start with line number 1000 and are incremented by 20.

RESET Command

Purpose:

To close all disk files and write the directory information to a diskette before it is removed from a disk drive.

Syntax:

RESET

Comments:

Always execute a RESET command before removing a diskette from a disk drive. Otherwise, when the diskette is used again, it will not have the current directory information written on the directory track.

RESET closes all open files on all drives and writes the directory track to every diskette with open files.

RESTORE Statement

Purpose:

To allow DATA statements to be reread from a specified line.

Syntax:

RESTORE[*line number*]

Comments:

If *line number* is specified, the next READ statement accesses the first item in the specified DATA statement.

If *line number* is omitted, the next READ statement accesses the first item in the first DATA statement.

Examples:

```
10 READ A,B,C,
20 RESTORE
30 READ D,E,F
40 DATA 57,68,79
 .
 .
 .
```

Assigns the value 57 to both A and D variables, 68 to B and E, and so on.

RESUME Statement

Purpose:

To continue program execution after an error-recovery procedure has been performed.

Syntax:

RESUME
RESUME 0
RESUME NEXT
RESUME *line number*

Comments:

Any one of the four formats shown above may be used, depending upon where execution is to resume:

Syntax	Result
RESUME or RESUME 0	Execution resumes at the statement that caused an error.
RESUME NEXT	Execution resumes at the statement immediately following the one that caused an error.
RESUME *line number*	Execution resumes at the specified line number.

A RESUME statement that is not in an error trapping routine causes a"RESUME without error" message to be printed.

Examples:

```
10 ON ERROR GOTO 900
 .
 .
 .
900 IF (ERR=230)AND(ERL=90) THEN PRINT "TRY AGAIN":RESUME 80
 .
 .
 .
```

If an error occurs after line 10 is executed, the action indicated in line 900
is taken and the program continues at line 80.

RETURN Statement

Purpose:

To return from a subroutine.

Syntax:

RETURN [*line number*]

Comments:

The RETURN statement causes GW-BASIC to branch back to the statement following the most recent GOSUB statement. A subroutine may contain more than one RETURN statement to return from different points in the subroutine. Subroutines may appear anywhere in the program.

RETURN *line number* is primarily intended for use with event trapping. It sends the event-trapping routine back into the GW-BASIC program at a fixed line number while still eliminating the GOSUB entry that the trap created.

When a trap is made for a particular event, the trap automatically causes a STOP on that event so that recursive traps can never take place. The RETURN from the trap routine automatically does an ON unless an explicit OFF has been performed inside the trap routine.

The nonlocal RETURN must be used with care. Any GOSUB, WHILE, or FOR statement active at the time of the trap remains active.

RIGHT$ FUNCTION

Purpose:

To return the rightmost *i* characters of string x$.

Syntax:

RIGHT$(x$,*i*)

Comments:

If *i* is equal to or greater than LEN(x$), RIGHT$ returns x$. If *i* equals zero, the null string (length zero) is returned (see the MID$ and LEFT$ functions).

Examples:

```
10 A$="DISK BASIC"
20 PRINT RIGHT$(A$,5)
RUN
BASIC
Ok
```

Prints the rightmost five characters in the A$ string.

RMDIR Command

Purpose:

To delete a subdirectory.

Syntax:

RMDIR *pathname*

Comments:

pathname is a string expression, not exceeding 63 characters, identifying the subdirectory to be removed from its parent.

The subdirectory to be deleted must be empty of all files except "." and ".." or a "Path file/access" error is given.

Examples:

Referring to the sample directory structure illustrated in CHDIR, the following command deletes the subdirectory *report*:

```
RMDIR "SALES\JOHN\REPORT"
```

278

RND Function

Purpose:

To return a random number between 0 and 1.

Syntax:

RND[(x)]

Comments:

The same sequence of random numbers is generated each time the program is run unless the random number generator is reseeded (see the RANDOMIZE statement). If x is equal to zero, then the last number is repeated.

If x is greater than 0, or if x is omitted, the next random number in the sequence is generated.

To get a random number within the range of zero through n, use the following formula:

INT(RND*(n + 1))

The random number generator may be seeded by using a negative value for x.

Examples:

```
10 FOR I=1 TO 5
20 PRINT INT(RND*101);
30 NEXT
RUN
53        30        31        51        5
Ok
```

Generates five pseudo-random numbers within the range of 0–100.

RUN Command

Purpose:

To execute the program currently in memory, or to load a file from the diskette into memory and run it.

Syntax:

RUN [*line number*][**,r**]
RUN *filename*[**,r**]

Comments:

RUN or RUN *line number* runs the program currently in memory.

If *line number* is specified, execution begins on that line. Otherwise, execution begins at the lower line number.

If there is no program in memory when RUN is executed, GW-BASIC returns to command level.

RUN *filename* closes all open files and deletes the current memory contents before loading the specified file from disk into memory and executing it.

The **r** option keeps all data files open.

If you are using the speaker on the computer, please note that executing the RUN command will turn off any sound that is currently running and will reset to Music Foreground. Also, the PEN and STRIG statements are reset to OFF.

Examples:

```
RUN NEWFIL,R
```

Runs NEWFIL without closing data files.

SAVE Command

Purpose:

To save a program file on diskette.

Syntax:

SAVE *filename*,**[,a]**
SAVE *filename*,**[,p]**

Comments:

filename is a quoted string that follows the normal MS-DOS naming conventions. If *filename* already exists, the file will be written over. If the extension is omitted, *.bas* will be used.

The **a** option saves the file in ASCII format. Otherwise, GW-BASIC saves the file in a compressed binary format. ASCII format takes more space on the diskette, but some diskette access commands (for example, the MERGE command and some MS-DOS commands, such as TYPE) may require an ASCII format file.

The **p** option protects the file by saving it in an encoded binary format. When a protected file is later run or loaded, any attempt to list or edit it fails. When the **p** option is used, make an additional copy under another name or diskette to facilitate future program maintenance.

Examples:

The following command saves the file *com2.bas* in the ASCII format:

```
SAVE COM2,A
```

The following command saves the file *prog.bas* in binary format, and protects access:

```
SAVE PROG,P
```

SCREEN Function

Purpose:

To return the ASCII code (0–255) for the character at the specified row (line) and column on the screen.

Syntax:

x = SCREEN(*row,col*[,*z*])

Comments:

x is a numeric variable receiving the ASCII code returned.

row is a valid numeric expression within the range 1 to 25.

col is a valid numeric expression 1 to 40, or 1 to 80, depending upon screen width setting. See the WIDTH statement.

z is a valid numeric expression with a true or false value. It may be used only in alpha mode.

The ordinal of the character at the specified coordinates is stored in the numeric variable. In alpha mode, if the optional parameter *z* is given and is true (nonzero), the color attribute for the character is returned instead of the ASCII code for the character (see the COLOR statement).

Any values entered outside of the range indicated result in an "Illegal function call" error. Row 25 may be referenced only if the function key is off.

Examples:

```
100 X=SCREEN (10,10)
```

If the character at 10,10 is A, then X is 65.

```
110 X= SCREEN (1,1,1)
```

Returns the color attribute of the character in the upper-left corner of the screen.

SCREEN Statement

Purpose:

To set the specifications for the display screen.

Syntax:

SCREEN [*mode*] [,[*colorswitch*]][,[*apage*]][,[*vpage*]]

Comments:

The SCREEN statement is chiefly used to select a screen mode appropriate for a particular display-hardware configuration. Supported hardware configurations and screen modes are described below.

MDPA with Monochrome Display: Mode 0

The IBM Monochrome Display and Printer Adapter (MDPA) is used to connect only to a monochrome display. Programs written for this configuration must be text mode only.

CGA with Color Display: Modes 0, 1, and 2

The IBM Color Graphics Adapter (CGA) and Color Display are typically paired with each other. This hardware configuration permits the running of text mode programs, and both medium-resolution and high-resolution graphics programs.

EGA with Color Display: Modes 0, 1, 2, 7, and 8

The five screen modes 0, 1, 2, 7, and 8 allow you to interface to the IBM Color Display when it is connected to an IBM Enhanced Graphics Adapter (EGA). If EGA switches are set for CGA compatibility, programs written for modes 1 and 2 will run just as they would with the CGA. Modes 7 and 8 are similar to modes 1 and 2, except that a wider range of colors is available in modes 7 and 8.

EGA with Enhanced Color Display: Modes 0, 1, 2, 7, and 8

With the EGA/IBM Enhanced Color Display configuration, modes 0, 1, 2, 7, and 8 are virtually identical to their EGA/Color Display counterparts. Two possible differences are as follows:

1. In mode 0, the border color cannot be the same as for the EGA/Color Display because the border cannot be set on an Enhanced Color Display when it is in 640 × 350 text mode.

2. The quality of the text is better on the Enhanced Color Display (an 8 × 14 character box for Enhanced Color Display versus an 8 × 8 character box for Color Display).

EGA with Enhanced Color Display: Mode 9

The full capability of the Enhanced Color Display is taken advantage of in this mode. Mode 9 allows the highest resolution possible for the EGA/Enhanced Color Display configuration. Programs written for this mode will not work for any other hardware configuration.

EGA with Monochrome Display: Mode 10

The IBM Monochrome Display can be used to display monochrome graphics at a very high resolution in this mode. Programs written for this mode will not work for any other hardware configuration.

Arguments

The *mode* argument is an integer expression with legal values 0, 1, 2, 7, 8, 9, and 10. All other values are illegal. Selection of a mode argument depends primarily on your program's anticipated display hardware, as described above.

Each of the SCREEN modes is described individually in the following paragraphs.

SCREEN 0

- Text mode only
- Either 40 × 25 or 80 × 25 text format with character-box size of 8 × 8 (8 × 14 with EGA)
- Assignment of 16 colors to any of 2 attributes
- Assignment of 16 colors to any of 16 attributes (with EGA)

SCREEN 1

- 320 × 200 pixel medium-resolution graphics
- 80 × 25 text format with character-box size of 8 × 8
- Assignment of 16 colors to any of 4 attributes
- Supports both EGA and CGA
- 2 bits per pixel

SCREEN 2

- 640 × 200 pixel high-resolution graphics
- 40 × 25 text format with character-box size of 8 × 8
- Assignment of 16 colors to any of 2 attributes
- Supports both EGA and CGA
- 1 bit per pixel

SCREEN 7

- 320 × 200 pixel medium-resolution graphics
- 40 × 25 text format with character-box size of 8 × 8
- 2, 4, or 8 memory pages with 64K, 128K, or 256K of memory, respectively, installed on the EGA
- Assignment of any of 16 colors to 16 attributes
- EGA required
- 4 bits per pixel

SCREEN 8

- 640 × 200 pixel high-resolution graphics
- 80 × 25 text format with character-box size of 8 × 8
- 1, 2, or 4 memory pages with 64K, 128K, or 256K of memory, respectively, installed on the EGA
- Assignment of any of 16 colors to 16 attributes
- EGA required
- 4 bits per pixel

SCREEN 9

- 640 × 350 pixel enhanced-resolution graphics
- 80 × 25 text format with character-box size of 8 × 14
- Assignment of either 64 colors to 16 attributes (more than 64K of EGA memory), or 16 colors to 4 attributes (64K of EGA memory)
- Two display pages if 256K of EGA memory installed
- EGA required
- 2 bits per pixel (64K EGA memory)
  4 bits per pixel (more than 64K EGA memory)

SCREEN 10

- 640 × 350 enhanced-resolution graphics
- 80 × 25 text format with character-box size of 8 × 14
- Two display pages if 256K of EGA memory installed
- Assignment of up to 9 pseudo-colors to 4 attributes.
- EGA required
- 2 bits per pixel

The following are default attributes for SCREEN 10, monochrome display:

Attribute Value	Displayed Pseudo-Color
0	Off
1	On, normal intensity
2	Blink
3	On, high intensity

The following are color values for SCREEN 10, monochrome display:

Color Value	Displayed Pseudo-Color
0	Off
1	Blink, off to on
2	Blink, off to high intensity
3	Blink, on to off
4	On
5	Blink, on to high intensity
6	Blink, high intensity to off
7	Blink, high intensity to on
8	High intensity

For both composite monitors and TVs, the *colorswitch* is a numeric expression that is either true (nonzero) or false (zero). A value of zero disables color and permits display of black and white images only. A nonzero value permits color. The meaning of the *colorswitch* argument is inverted in SCREEN mode 0.

For hardware configurations that include an EGA and enough memory to support multiple-screen pages, two arguments are available. These *apage* and *vpage* arguments determine the "active" and "visual" memory pages. The active page is the area in memory where graphics statements are written; the visual page is the area of memory that is displayed on the screen.

Animation can be achieved by alternating the display of graphics pages. The goal is to display the visual page with completed graphics output, while executing graphics statements in one or more active pages. A page is displayed only when graphics output to that page is complete. Thus, the following program fragment is typical:

```
SCREEN 7,,1,2    'work in page 1, show page 2
.
.    Graphics output to page 1
.    while viewing page 2
.
SCREEN 7,,2,1    'work in page 2, show page 1
.
.    Graphics output to page 2
.    while viewing page 1
.
```

The number of pages available depends on the SCREEN mode and the amount of available memory, as described in the following table:

Table 2

SCREEN Mode Specifications

Mode	Resolution	Attribute Range	Color Range	EGA Memory	Pages	Page Size
0	40 – column text	NA	$0-15^a$	NA	1	2K
	80 – column text	NA	$0-15^a$	NA	1	4K
1	320×200	$0-3^b$	$0-3$	NA	1	16K
2	640×200	$0-1^b$	$0-1$	NA	1	16K
7	320×200	$0-15$	$0-15$	64K	2	32K
				128K	4	
				256K	8	
8	640×200	$0-15$	$0-15$	64K	1	64K
				128K	2	
				256K	4	
9	640×350	$0-3$	$0-15$	64K	1	64K
		$0-15$	$0-63$	128K	1	128K
		$0-15$	$0-63$	256K	2	
10	640×350	$0-3$	$0-8$	128K	1	128K
				256K	2	

[a] Numbers in the range 16–31 are blinking versions of the colors 0–15.
[b] Attributes applicable only with EGA.

Attributes and Colors

For various screen modes and display hardware configurations, different attribute and color settings exist. (See the PALETTE statement for a discussion of attribute and color number.) The majority of these attribute and color configurations are summarized in the following table:

Table 3

Default Attributes and Colors for Most Screen Modes

Attributes for Mode			Color Display		Monochrome Display	
1,9	2	0,7,8,9[b]	Number[c]	Color	Number[c]	Color
0	0	0	0	Black	0	Off
		1	1	Blue		(Underlined) [a]
		2	2	Green	1	On [a]
		3	3	Cyan	1	On [a]
		4	4	Red	1	On [a]
		5	5	Magenta	1	On [a]
		6	6	Brown	1	On [a]
		7	7	White	1	On [a]
		8	8	Gray	0	Off
		9	9	Light Blue		High intensity (underlined)
		10	10	Light Green	2	High intensity
1		11	11	Light Cyan	2	High intensity
		12	12	Light Red	2	High intensity
2		13	13	Light Magenta	2	High intensity
		14	14	Yellow	2	High intensity
3	1	15	15	High-intensity White	0	Off

[a] Off when used for background.
[b] With EGA memory > 64K.
[c] Only for mode 0 monochrome.

The default foreground colors for the various modes are given in the following table:

Table 4

Default Foreground Colors

	Default foreground attribute		Default foreground color	
Screen mode	**Color/Extended[a] Display**	**Monochrome Display**	**Color/Extended[a] Display**	**Monochrome Display**
0	7	7	7	1
1	3	NA	15	NA
2	1	NA	15	NA
7	15	NA	15	NA
8	15	NA	15	NA
9	3[b]	NA	63	NA
10	NA	3	NA	8

[a] IBM Enhanced Color Display
[b] 15 if greater than 64K of EGA memory
NA = Not Applicable

SGN Function

Purpose:

To return the sign of x.

Syntax:

SGN(x)

Comments:

x is any numeric expression.

If x is positive, SGN(x) returns 1.
If x is 0, SGN(x) returns 0.
If x is negative, SGN(x) returns -1.

This statement is similar to, but not the same as, SIN(x), which returns a trigonometric function in radians, rather than in ones and zeros.

Examples:

```
10 INPUT "Enter value",x
20 ON SGN(X)+2 GOTO 100,200,300
```

GW-BASIC branches to 100 if X is negative, 200 if X is 0, and 300 if X is positive.

SHELL Statement

Purpose:

To load and execute another program or batch file. When the program finishes, control returns to the GW-BASIC program at the statement following the SHELL statement. A program executed under the control of GW-BASIC is referred to as a *child process*.

Syntax:

SHELL [*string*]

Comments:

string is a valid string expression containing the name of a program to run and (optionally) command arguments.

The program name in *string* may have any extension that MS-DOS COMMAND.COM supports. If no extension is supplied, COMMAND will look for a .COM file, then an .EXE file, and finally, a .BAT file. If none is found, SHELL will issue a "File not found" error.

Any text separated from the program name by at least one blank space will be processed by COMMAND as program parameters.

GW-BASIC remains in memory while the child process is running. When the child process finishes, GW-BASIC continues at the statement following the SHELL statement.

SHELL with no string will go to MS-DOS. You may now do anything that COMMAND allows. When ready to return to GW-BASIC, type the MS-DOS command EXIT.

Examples:

```
SHELL
A>DIR
A>EXIT
Ok
```

Write some data to be sorted, use SHELL SORT to sort it, then read the sorted data to write a report.

```
10    OPEN "SORTIN.DAT" FOR OUTPUT AS #1
20    'write data to be sorted
   .
   .
   .
1000  CLOSE 1
1010  SHELL  "SORT <SORTIN.DAT  >SORTOUT.DAT"
1020  OPEN "SORTOUT.DAT" FOR INPUT AS #1
1030   'Process the sorted data
```

SIN Function

Purpose:

To calculate the trigonometric sine of x, in radians.

Syntax:

SIN(x)

Comments:

SIN(x) is calculated in single-precision unless the **/d** switch is used when GW-BASIC is executed.

To obtain SIN(x) when x is in degrees, use SIN($x*\pi/180$).

Examples:

```
PRINT SIN(1.5)
.9974951
Ok
```

The sine of 1.5 radians is .9974951 (single-precision).

SOUND Statement

Purpose:

To generate sound through the speaker.

Syntax:

SOUND *freq,duration*

Comments:

freq is the desired frequency in Hertz (cycles per second). *freq* is a numeric expression within the range of 37 to 32767.

duration is the desired duration in clock ticks. Clock ticks occur 18.2 times per second. *duration* must be a numeric expression within the range of 0 to 65535.

Values below .022 produce an infinite sound until the next SOUND or PLAY statement is executed.

If *duration* is zero, any active SOUND statement is turned off. If no SOUND statement is running, a *duration* of zero has no effect.

The sound is executed in foreground or background depending on the PLAY statement.

Examples:

The following example creates random sounds of short duration:

```
2500 SOUND RND*1000+37,2
2600 GOTO 2500
```

The following table shows the relationship of notes and their frequencies in the two octaves adjacent to middle C.

Table 5

Relationships of Notes and Frequencies

Note	Frequency	Note	Frequency
C	130.810	C*	523.250
D	146.830	D	587.330
E	164.810	E	659.260
F	174.610	F	698.460
G	196.000	G	783.990
A	220.000	A	880.000
B	246.940	B	987.770
C	261.630	C	1046.500
D	293.660	D	1174.700
E	329.630	E	1318.500
F	349.230	F	1396.900
G	392.000	G	1568.000
A	440.000	A	1760.000
B	493.880	B	1975.500

*Middle C.

By doubling or halving the frequency, the coinciding note values can be estimated for the preceding and following octaves.

To produce periods of silence, use the following statement:

SOUND 32767, *duration*

To calculate the duration of one beat, divide beats per minute into the number of clock ticks in a minute (1092).

The following table illustrates tempos requested by clock ticks:

Table 6

Tempos Requested by Clock Ticks

Tempo	Notation	Beats/ Minute	Ticks/ Beat
very slow	Larghissimo		
	Largo	40–66	27.3–18.2
	Larghetto	60–66	18.2–16.55
	Grave		
	Lento		
	Adagio	66–76	16.55–14.37
slow	Adagietto		
	Andante	76–108	14.37–10.11
medium	Andantino		
	Moderato	108–120	10.11–9.1
fast	Allegretto		
	Allegro	120–168	9.1–6.5
	Vivace		
	Veloce		
	Presto	168-208	6.5–5.25
very fast	Prestissimo		

SPACE$ Function

Purpose:

To return a string of x spaces.

Syntax:

SPACE$(x)

Comments:

x is rounded to an integer and must be within the range of 0 to 255 (see the SPC function).

Examples:

```
10 FOR N=1 TO 5
20 X$=SPACE$(N)
30 PRINT X$;N
40 NEXT N
RUN
1
  2
   3
     4
      5
Ok
```

Line 20 adds one space for each loop execution.

SPC Function

Purpose:

To skip a specified number of spaces in a PRINT or an LPRINT statement.

Syntax:

SPC(*n*)

Comments:

n must be within the range of 0 to 255.

If *n* is greater than the defined width of the printer or the screen, the value used will be *n* MOD width.

A semicolon is assumed to follow the SPC(*n*) command.

SPC can only be used with the PRINT, LPRINT, and PRINT# statements (see the SPACE$ function).

Examples:

```
PRINT "OVER" SPC(15) "THERE"
OVER            THERE
Ok
```

SQR Function

Purpose:

Returns the square root of x.

Syntax:

SQR(x)

Comments:

x must be greater than or equal to 0.

SQR(x) is computed in single-precision unless the /d switch is used when GW-BASIC is executed.

Examples:

```
10 FOR X=10 TO 25 STEP 5
20 PRINT X; SQR(X)
30 NEXT
RUN
10      3.162278
15      3.872984
20      4.472136
25      5
Ok
```

STICK Function

Purpose:

To return the x and y coordinates of two joysticks.

Syntax:

x = STICK(_n_**)**

Comments:

x is a numeric variable for storing the result.

_n_ is a valid numeric expression within the range of 0 to 3.

Value of _n_	Coordinate Returned
0	x coordinate of joystick A. Stores the x and y values for both joysticks for the following three function calls.
1	y coordinate of joystick A.
2	x coordinate of joystick B.
3	y coordinate of joystick B.

STOP Statement

Purpose:

To terminate program execution and return to command level.

Syntax:

STOP

Comments:

STOP statements may be used anywhere in a program to terminate execution. When a STOP is encountered, the following message is printed:

```
Break in line nnnnn
```

Unlike the END statement, the STOP statement does not close files.

GW-BASIC always returns to command level after a STOP is executed. Execution is resumed by issuing a CONT command.

Examples:

```
10  INPUT A,B,C
20  K=A^2*5.3:L=B^3/.26
30  STOP
40  M=C*K+100:PRINT M
RUN
? 1,2,3
BREAK IN 30
Ok
PRINT L
30.76923
Ok
CONT
115.9
Ok
```

STR$ Function

Purpose:

To return a string representation of the value of x.

Syntax:

STR$(x)

Comments:

STR$(x) is the complementary function to VAL(x$) (see the VAL function).

Examples:

```
5 REM ARITHMETIC FOR KIDS
10 INPUT "TYPE A NUMBER";N
20 ON LEN(STR$(N)) GOSUB 30,40,50
  .
  .
  .
```

This program branches to various subroutines, depending on the number of characters typed before the RETURN key is pressed.

STRIG Statement and Function

Purpose:

To return the status of the joystick triggers.

Syntax:

As a statement:

STRIG ON
STRIG OFF

As a function:

x = STRIG(n)

Comments:

x is a numeric variable for storing the result.

n is a valid numeric expression within the range of 0 to 7.

STRIG ON must be executed before any STRIG(n) function calls may be made. Once STRIG ON is executed, GW-BASIC will check to see if a button has been pressed before every statement is executed. STRIG OFF disables the checking.

n is a numeric expression within the range of 0 to 7 that returns the following values:

Value of n	Returns
0	−1 if trigger A1 was pressed since the last STRIG(0) statement; returns 0, if not.
1	−1 if trigger A1 is currently pressed; returns 0, if not.
2	−1 if trigger B1 was pressed since the last STRIG(2) statement; returns 0, if not.

3	−1 if trigger B1 is currently pressed; returns 0, if not.
4	−1 if trigger A2 was pressed since the last STRIG(4) statement; returns 0, if not.
5	−1 if trigger A2 is currently pressed; returns 0, if not.

STRIG(n) Statement

Purpose:

To allow the use of a joystick by enabling or disabling the trapping of its buttons.

Syntax:

STRIG(*n*) **ON**
STRIG(*n*) **OFF**
STRIG(*n*) **STOP**

Comments:

n is 0, 2, 4, or 6, corresponding to the buttons on the joystick, where

0 is button A1
2 is button B1
4 is button A2
6 is button B2

Examples:

STRIG(*n*) **ON**

Enables trapping of the joystick buttons. After this statement is executed, GW-BASIC checks to see if this button has been pressed before executing following statements.

STRIG(*n*) **OFF**

Disables GW-BASIC from checking the state of the button.

STRIG(*n*) **STOP**

Disables trapping of a given button through the ON STRIG(*n*) statement. But any pressings are remembered so that trapping may take place once it is re-enabled.

STRING$ Function

Purpose:

To return

- a string of length n whose characters all have ASCII code j, or
- the first character of x$

Syntax:

**STRING$**($n,j$)
STRING$**($n,x$**$)

Comments:

STRING$ is also useful for printing top and bottom borders on the screen or the printer.

n and j are integer expressions in the range of 0 to 255.

Examples:

```
10 X$ = STRING$(10,45)
20 PRINT X$ "MONTHLY REPORT" X$
RUN
----------MONTHLY REPORT----------
Ok
```

45 is the decimal equivalent of the ASCII symbol for the minus $(-)$ sign.

Appendix C lists ASCII character codes.

SWAP Statement

Purpose:

To exchange the values of two variables.

Syntax:

SWAP *variable1,variable2*

Comments:

Any type variable may be swapped (integer, single-precision, double-precision, string), but the two variables must be of the same type or a "Type mismatch" error results.

Examples:

```
LIST
10 A$="ONE ":B$="ALL ":C$="FOR "
20 PRINT A$ C$ B$
30 SWAP A$, B$
40 PRINT A$ C$ B$
RUN
Ok
ONE FOR ALL
ALL FOR ONE
Ok
```

Line 30 swaps the values in the A$ and B$ strings.

SYSTEM Command

Purpose:

To return to MS-DOS.

Syntax:

SYSTEM

Comments:

Save your program before pressing RETURN, or the program will be lost.

The SYSTEM command closes all the files before it returns to MS-DOS. If you entered GW-BASIC through a batch file from MS-DOS, the SYSTEM command returns you to the batch file, which continues executing at the point it left off.

Examples:

```
SYSTEM
A>
```

TAB Function

Purpose:

Spaces to position *n* on the screen.

Syntax:

TAB(n)

Comments:

If the current print position is already beyond space *n*, TAB goes to that position on the next line.

Space 1 is the leftmost position. The rightmost position is the screen width.

n must be within the range of 1 to 255.

If the TAB function is at the end of a list of data items, GW-BASIC will not return the cursor to the next line. It is as though the TAB function has an implied semicolon after it.

TAB may be used only in PRINT, LPRINT, or PRINT# statements (see the SPC function).

Examples:

```
10 PRINT "NAME" TAB(25) "AMOUNT": PRINT
20 READ A$,B$
30 PRINT A$ TAB(25) B$
40 DATA "G. T. JONES","$25.00"
RUN
NAME            AMOUNT

G. T. JONES     $25.00
Ok
```

TAN Function

Purpose:

To calculate the trigonometric tangent of x, in radians.

Syntax:

TAN(x)

Comments:

TAN(x) is calculated in single-precision unless the /**d** switch is used when GW-BASIC is executed.

If TAN overflows, the "Overflow" error message is displayed; machine infinity with the appropriate sign is supplied as the result, and execution continues.

To obtain TAN(x) when x is in degrees, use TAN($x*\pi/180$).

Examples:

```
10 Y = TAN(X)
```

When executed, Y will contain the value of the tangent of X radians.

TIME$ Statement and Variable

Purpose:

To set or retrieve the current time.

Syntax:

As a statement:

TIME$ = *string exp*

As a variable:

string exp = **TIME$**

Comments:

string exp is a valid string literal or variable that lets you set hours (*hh*), hours and minutes (*hh:mm*), or hours, minutes, and seconds (*hh:mm:ss*).

hh sets the hour (0–23). Minutes and seconds default to 00.

hh:mm sets the hour and minutes (0–59). Seconds default to 00.

hh:mm:ss sets the hour, minutes, and seconds (0–59).

If *string exp* is not a valid string, a "Type mismatch" error results.

As you enter any of the above values, you may omit the leading zero, if any. You must, however, enter at least one digit. If you wanted to set the time as a half hour after midnight, you could enter TIME$ = "0:30", but not TIME$ = ":30".

If any of the values are out of range, an "Illegal function call" error is issued. The previous time is retained.

The current time is stored if TIME$ is the target of a string assignment.

The current time is fetched and assigned to the string variable if TIME$ is the expression in a LET or PRINT statement.

If *string exp* = TIME$, TIME$ returns an 8-character string in the form *hh:mm:ss*.

Examples:

The following example sets the time at 8:00 A.M.:

```
TIME$ = "08:00"
Ok
PRINT TIME$
08:00:05
Ok
```

The following program displays the current date and time on the 25th line of the screen and will sound on the minute and half minute.

```
10 KEY OFF:SCREEN 0:WIDTH 80:CLS
20 LOCATE 25,5
30 PRINT DATE$,TIME$;
40 SEC=VAL(MID$(TIME$,7,2))
50 IF SEC=SSEC THEN 20 ELSE SSEC=SEC
60 IF SEC=0 THEN 1010
70 IF SEC=30 THEN 1020
80 IF SEC<57 THEN 20

1000 SOUND 1000,2:GOTO 20
1010 SOUND 2000,8:GOTO 20
1020 SOUND 400,4:GOTO 20
```

TIMER Function

Purpose:

To return single-precision floating-point numbers representing the elapsed number of seconds since midnight or system reset.

Syntax:

v = TIMER

Comments:

Fractions of seconds are calculated to the nearest degree possible. TIMER is read-only.

TRON/TROFF Commands

Purpose:

To trace the execution of program statements.

Syntax:

TRON
TROFF

Comments:

As an aid in debugging, the TRON (trace on) command enables a trace flag that prints each line number of the program as it is executed. The numbers appear enclosed in square brackets.

TRON may be executed in either the direct or indirect mode.

The trace flag is disabled with the TROFF (trace off) command, or when a NEW command is executed.

Examples:

```
TRON
Ok
10 K=10
20 FOR J=1 TO 2
30 L=K + 10
40 PRINT J;K;L
50 K=K+10
60 NEXT
70 END
RUN
[10][20][30][40]  1  10  20
[50][60][30][40]  2  20  30
[50][60][70]
Ok
TROFF
Ok
```

UNLOCK Statement

Purpose:

To release locks that have been applied to an opened file. This is used in a multi-device environment, often referred to as a *network* or *network environment*.

Syntax:

UNLOCK [**#**]*n* [,[*record number*] [**TO** *record number*]]

Comments

n is the number that was assigned to the file as it was originally numbered in the program.

record number is the number of the individual record that is to be unlocked. Or, if a range of records are to be unlocked, *record number* designates the beginning and ending record of the specified range.

The range of legal record numbers is 1 to $2^{32} - 1$. The limit on record size is 32767 bytes.

The record range specified must be from lower to (the same or) higher record numbers.

If a starting record number is not specified, the record number 1 is assumed.

If an ending record number is not specified, then only the specified record is unlocked.

The following are legal UNLOCK statements:

UNLOCK #*n*	unlocks the entire file *n*
UNLOCK #*n*, X	unlocks record X only
UNLOCK #*n*, TO Y	unlocks records 1 through Y
UNLOCK #*n*, X TO Y	unlocks records X through Y

The locked file or record range should be unlocked before the file is closed.

Failure to execute the UNLOCK statement can jeopardize future access to that file in a network environment.

In the case of files opened in random mode, if a range of record numbers is specified, this range must match exactly the record number range given in the LOCK statement.

The "Permission denied" message will appear if a syntactically correct UNLOCK request cannot be granted. The UNLOCK statement must match exactly the paired LOCK statement.

It is expected that the time in which files or regions within files are locked will be short, and thus the suggested usage of the LOCK statement is within short-term paired LOCK/UNLOCK statements.

Examples:

The following demonstrates how the LOCK/UNLOCK statements should be used:

```
LOCK #1, 1 TO 4
LOCK #1, 5 TO 8
UNLOCK #1, 1 TO 4
UNLOCK #1, 5 TO 8
```

The following example is illegal:

```
LOCK #1, 1 TO 4
LOCK #1, 5 TO 8
UNLOCK #1, 1 TO 8
```

USR Function

Purpose:

To call an assembly language subroutine.

Syntax:

v = USR[n](argument)

Comments:

n specifies which USR routine is being called.

argument can be any numeric or string expression.

Although the CALL statement is recommended for calling assembly language subroutines, the USR function call may also be used. See Appendix D for a comparison of CALL and USR and for a detailed discussion of calling assembly language subroutines.

Only values 0–9 are valid for n. If n is omitted, USR0 is assumed (see DEF USR for the rules governing n).

If a segment other than the default segment (GW-BASIC data segment, DS) is used, a DEF SEG statement must be executed prior to a USR call. This ensures that the code segment points to the subroutine being called.

The segment address given in the DEF SEG statement determines the starting segment of the subroutine.

For each USR function, a corresponding DEF USR statement must have been executed to define the USR call offset. This offset and the currently active DEF SEG segment address determine the starting address of the subroutine.

If more than 10 user routines are required, the value(s) of DEF USR may be redefined for the other starting addresses as many times as needed.

The type (numeric or string) of the variable receiving the function call must be consistent with the argument passed. If no argument is required by the assembly language routine, then a dummy argument must be supplied.

VAL Function

Purpose:

Returns the numerical value of string x$.

Syntax:

VAL(x$)

Comments:

The VAL function also strips leading blanks, tabs, and line feeds from the argument string. For example, the following line returns -3:

```
VAL(" -3")
```

The STR$ function (for numeric to string conversion) is the complement to the VAL(x$) function.

If the first character of x$ is not numeric, the VAL(x$) function will return zero.

Examples:

```
10 READ NAME$,CITY$,STATE$,ZIP$
20 IF VAL(ZIP$)<90000 OR VAL(ZIP$)>96699 THEN
PRINT NAME$ TAB(25) "OUT OF STATE"
30 IF VAL(ZIP$)>=90801 AND VAL(ZIP$)<=90815 THEN
PRINT NAME$ TAB(25) "LONG BEACH"
 .
 .
 .
```

VARPTR Function

Purpose:

To return the address in memory of the variable or file control block (FCB).

Syntax:

VARPTR(*variable name*)
VARPTR(*#file number*)

Comments:

VARPTR is usually used to obtain the address of a variable or array so it can be passed to an assembly language subroutine. A function call of the following form:

```
VARPTR(A(0))
```

is usually specified when passing an array, so that the lowest-addressed element of the array is returned.

All simple variables should be assigned before calling VARPTR for an array, because the addresses of the arrays change whenever a new simple variable is assigned.

VARPTR (*#file number*) returns the starting address of the GW-BASIC File Control Block assigned to file number.

VARPTR (*variable name*) returns the address of the first byte of data identified with the variable name.

A value must be assigned to variable name prior to execution of VARPTR; otherwise, an "Illegal function call" error results.

Any type variable name may be used (numeric, string, or array), and the address returned will be an integer within the range of 32767 to −32768. If a negative address is returned, it is added to 65536 to obtain the actual address.

Offsets to information in the FCB from the address returned by VARPTR are shown in the following table:

Table 7

Offsets to FCB Information

Offset	Length	Name	Description
0	1	Mode	The mode in which the file was opened: 1 Input only 2 Output only 4 Random I/O 16 Append only 32 Internal use 64 Future use 128 Internal use
1	38	FCB	Diskette file control block.
39	2	CURLOC	Number of sectors read or written for sequential access. The last record number +1 read or written for random files.
41	1	ORNOFS	Number of bytes in sector when read or written.
42	1	NMLOFS	Number of bytes left in INPUT buffer.
43	3	***	Reserved for future expansion.
46	1	DEVICE	Device Number: 0-9 Disks A: through J: 255 KYBD: 254 SCRN: 253 LPT1: 252 CAS1: 251 COM1: 250 COM2: 249 LPT2: 248 LPT3:
47	1	WIDTH	Device width.
48	1	POS	Position in buffer for PRINT.
49	1	FLAGS	Internal use during BLOAD/BSAVE. Not used for data files.
50	1	OUTPOS	Output position used during tab expansion.

51	128	BUFFER	Physical data buffer. Used to transfer data between DOS and BASIC. Use this offset to examine data in sequential I/O mode.
179	2	VRECL	Variable length record size. Default is 128. Set by length option in OPEN statement.
181	2	PHYREC	Current physical record number.
183	2	LOGREC	Current logical record number.
185	1	***	Future use.
186	2	OUTPOS	Disk files only. Output position for PRINT, INPUT, and WRITE.
188	n	FIELD	Actual FIELD data buffer. Size is determined by S: switch. VRECL bytes are transferred between BUFFER and FIELD on I/O operations. Use this offset to examine file data in random I/O mode.

Example 1:

```
100 X=VARPTR(Y)
```

When executed, the variable X will contain an address that points to the storage space assigned to the variable Y.

Example 2:

```
10 OPEN "DATA.FIL" AS #1
20 FCBADR = VARPTR(#1)
30 DATADR = FCBADR+188
40 A$ = PEEK(DATADR)
```

In line 20, FCBADR contains the start of FCB.

In line 30, DATADR contains the address of the data buffer.

In line 40, A$ contains the first byte in the data buffer.

VARPTR$ Function

Purpose:

To return a character form of the offset of a variable in memory.

Syntax:

VARPTR$(*variable*)

Comments:

variable is the name of a variable that exists in the program.

Note

> Assign all simple variables before calling VARPTR$ for an array element, because the array addresses change when a new simple variable is assigned.

VARPTR$ returns a three-byte string of the following form:

Byte 0	Byte 1	Byte 2

Byte 0 contains one of the following variable types:

2	integer
3	string
4	single-precision
8	double-precision

Byte 1 contains the 8086 address format, and is the least significant byte.
Byte 2 contains the 8086 address format, and is the most significant byte.

Examples:

```
100 X = USR(VARPTR$(Y))
```

VIEW Statement

Purpose:

To define a physical viewport limit from x1,y1 (upper-left x,y coordinates) to x2,y2 (lower-right x,y coordinates).

Syntax:

VIEW [[SCREEN][(*x1,y1*)-(*x2,y2*) [,[*fill*][,[*border*]]]]

Comments:

RUN or VIEW with no arguments define the entire screen as the viewport.

(*x1,y1*) are the upper-left coordinates.

(*x2,y2*) are the lower-right coordinates.

The *fill* attribute lets you fill the view area with color.

The *border* attribute lets you draw a line surrounding the viewport if space for a border is available. If border is omitted, no border is drawn.

The *x* and *y* coordinates must be within the physical bounds of the screen and must define the rectangle within the screen that graphics map into. The *x* and *y* coordinate pairs will be sorted, with the smallest values placed first.

Points are plotted relative to the viewpoint if the screen argument is omitted; that is, *x1* and *y1* are added to the *x* and *y* coordinates before the point is plotted.

It is possible to have a varied number of pairs of *x* and *y*. The only restriction is that *x1* cannot equal *x2*, and *y1* cannot equal *y2*.

Points are plotted absolutely if the SCREEN argument is present. Only points within the current viewpoint will be plotted.

When using VIEW, the CLS statement clears only the current viewport. To clear the entire screen, you must use VIEW to disable the viewports. Then use CLS to clear the screen. CLS does not move the cursor to home. Press CTRL-HOME to send the cursor home, and clear the screen.

Examples:

The following defines a viewport such that the statement PSET(0,0),3 would set down a point at the physical screen location 10,10.

```
VIEW (10,10)-(200,100)
```

The following defines a viewport such that the point designated by the statement PSET(0,0),3 would not appear because 0,0 is outside of the viewport. PSET(10,10),3 would be within the viewport.

```
VIEW SCREEN (10,10)-(200,100)
```

VIEW PRINT Statement

Purpose:

To set the boundaries of the screen text window.

Syntax:

VIEW PRINT [*topline* **TO** *bottomline*]

Comments:

VIEW PRINT without *topline* and *bottomline* parameters initializes the whole screen area as the text window. The whole screen area consists of lines 1 to 24; by default, line 25 is not used.

Statements and functions that operate within the defined text window include CLS, LOCATE, PRINT, and SCREEN.

The screen editor will limit functions such as scroll and cursor movement to the text window.

For more information, see VIEW.

327

WAIT Statement

Purpose:

To suspend program execution while monitoring the status of a machine input port.

Syntax:

WAIT *port number*, *n*[,*j*]

Comments:

port number represents a valid machine port number within the range of 0 to 65535.

n and *j* are integer expressions in the range of 0 to 255.

The WAIT statement causes execution to be suspended until a specified machine input port develops a specified bit pattern.

The data read at the port is XORed with the integer expression *j*, and then ANDed with *n*.

If the result is zero, GW-BASIC loops back and reads the data at the port again. If the result is nonzero, execution continues with the next statement.

When executed, the WAIT statement tests the byte *n* for set bits. If any of the bits is set, then the program continues with the next statement in the program. WAIT does not wait for an entire pattern of bits to appear, but only for one of them to occur.

It is possible to enter an infinite loop with the WAIT statement. You can exit the loop by pressing CTRL-BREAK, or by resetting the system.

If *j* is omitted, zero is assumed.

Examples:

```
100 WAIT 32,2
```

Suspends machine operation until port 32 receives 2 as input.

WHILE-WEND Statement

Purpose:

To execute a series of statements in a loop as long as a given condition
is true.

Syntax:

WHILE *expression*

.

.

.

[*loop statements*]

.

.

.

WEND

Comments:

If *expression* is nonzero (true), loop statements are executed until the
WEND statement is encountered. GW-BASIC then returns to the WHILE
statement and checks *expression*. If it is still true, the process is repeated.

If it is not true, execution resumes with the statement following the WEND
statement.

WHILE and WEND loops may be nested to any level. Each WEND matches
the most recent WHILE.

An unmatched WHILE statement causes a "WHILE without WEND" error.
An unmatched WEND statement causes a "WEND without WHILE" error.

WHILE-WEND Statement

Examples:

```
90 'BUBBLE SORT ARRAY A$
100 FLIPS=1
110 WHILE FLIPS
115 FLIPS=0
120 FOR N=1 TO J-1
130 IF A$(N)>A$(N+1) THEN SWAP A$(N),A$(N+1):FLIPS=1
140 NEXT N
150 WEND
```

WIDTH Statement

Purpose:

To set the printed line width in number of characters for the screen and line printer.

Syntax:

WIDTH *size*
WIDTH *file number*, *size*
WIDTH **"***dev***"**, *size*

Comments:

size, an integer within the range of 0 to 255, is the new width.

file number is the number of the file that is open.

dev is a valid string expression identifying the device. Valid devices are SCRN:, LPT1:, LPT2:, LPT3:, COM1:, and COM2:.

Changing Screen Width

The following statements are used to set the screen width. Only a 40- or 80-column width is allowed.

WIDTH *size*
WIDTH **"SCRN:"**,*size*

See the SCREEN statement for more information.

Changing SCREEN mode affects screen width only when moving between SCREEN 2 and SCREEN 1 or SCREEN 0.

Note

> Changing the screen width clears the screen and sets the border screen color to black.

Changing Lineprinter Width

The following WIDTH statement is used as a deferred width assignment for the lineprinter. This statement stores the new width value without actually changing the current width setting:

```
WIDTH "LPT1:",size
```

A statement of the following form recognizes this stored width value:

```
OPEN "LPT1:" FOR OUTPUT AS number
```

and uses it while the file is open:

```
WIDTH file number,size
```

If the file is open to **lpt1:**, lineprinter width is immediately changed to the new size specified. This allows the width to be changed at will while the file is open. This form of WIDTH has meaning only for **lpt1:**. After outputting the indicated number of characters from the open file, GW-BASIC inserts a carriage return at the end of the line and wraps the output, if the width is less than the length of the record.

Valid widths for the lineprinter are 1 through 255.

Specifying WIDTH 255 for the lineprinter (**lpt1**:) enables line wrapping. This has the effect of infinite width.

Any value entered outside of these ranges results in an "Illegal function call" error. The previous value is retained.

Using the WIDTH statement on a communications file causes a carriage return to be sent after the number of characters specified by the *size* attribute. It does not alter either the receive or transmit buffer.

Examples:

```
10 WIDTH "LPT1:",75
20 OPEN "LPT1:" FOR OUTPUT AS #1
  .
  .
  .
6020 WIDTH #1,40
```

Line 10 stores a line printer width of 75 characters per line.

Line 20 opens file #1 to the line printer and sets the width to 75 for subsequent PRINT #1, statements.

Line 6020 changes the current line printer width to 40 characters per line.

WINDOW Statement

Purpose:

To draw lines, graphics, and objects in space not bounded by the physical limits of the screen.

Syntax:

WINDOW[[SCREEN](x1,y1)-(x2,y2)]

Comments:

(x1,y1) and (x2,y2) are the coordinates defined by the user. These coordinates, called the *world coordinates*, may be any single-precision, floating-point number. They define the world coordinate space that graphics statements map into the physical coordinate space, as defined by the VIEW statement.

WINDOW is the rectangular region in the world coordinate space. It allows zoom and pan. It allows the user to draw lines, graphics, and objects in space not bounded by the physical limits of the screen. To do this the user specifies the world coordinate pairs (x1,y1) and (x2,y2). GW-BASIC then converts the world coordinate pairs into the appropriate physical coordinate pairs for subsequent display within screen space.

WINDOW inverts, with the screen attribute omitted, the y coordinate on subsequent graphics statements. This places the (x1,y1) coordinate in the lower-left and the (x1,y2) coordinate in the upper-right corner of the screen. This allows the screen to be viewed in true Cartesian coordinates.

The coordinates are not inverted when the SCREEN attribute is included. This places the (x1,y1) coordinate in the upper-left corner and the (x2,y2) coordinate in the lower-right corner of the screen.

The WINDOW statement sorts the x and y argument pairs into ascending order. For example

```
WINDOW (50,50)-(10,10)
```

becomes

```
WINDOW (10,10)-(50,50)
```

Or

```
WINDOW (-2,2)-(2,-2)
```

becomes

```
WINDOW (-2,-2)-(2,2)
```

All coordinate pairs of *x* and *y* are valid, except that *x1* cannot equal *x2* and *y1* cannot equal *y2*.

WINDOW with no arguments disables previous window statements.

Example 1:

If you type the following:

```
NEW
SCREEN 2
```

the screen uses the standard coordinate attributes as follows:

```
0,0320,0639,0

\/y increases
320,100

0,199320,100639,199
```

Example 2:

If you type the following:

```
WINDOW (-1,-1)-(1,1)
```

the screen uses the Cartesian coordinates as defined in the following statement:

```
-1,10,11,1
/\y increases

0,0

\/y decreases
-1,10,11,1
```

Example 3:

If you type the following:

```
WINDOW SCREEN (-1,-1)-(1,1)
```

the screen uses the non-inverted coordinate as defined in the following statement:

```
-1,-10,-11,-1
/y decreases

0,0

\/y increases
-1,10,11,1
```

RUN, SCREEN, and WINDOW with no attributes disable any WINDOW definitions and return the screen to its normal physical coordinates.

WRITE Statement

Purpose:

To output data to the screen.

Syntax:

WRITE[*list of expressions*]

Comments:

If *list of expressions* is omitted, a blank line is output. If *list of expressions* is included, the values of the expressions are output at the terminal. The expressions in the list may be numeric and/or string expressions, and must be separated by commas or semicolons.

When printed items are output, each item will be separated from the last by a comma. Printed strings are delimited by double quotation marks. After the last item in the list is printed, GW-BASIC inserts a carriage return/line feed.

The difference between WRITE and PRINT is that WRITE inserts commas between displayed items and delimits strings with double quotation marks. Positive numbers are not preceded by blank spaces.

WRITE outputs numeric values using the same format as the PRINT statement.

Examples:

```
10 A=80:B=90:C$="THAT'S ALL"
20 WRITE A,B,C$
RUN
80, 90,"THAT'S ALL"
Ok
```

WRITE# Statement

Purpose:

To write data to a sequential file.

Syntax:

WRITE #*filenum*, *list of expressions*

Comments:

filenum is the number under which the file was opened for output.

list of expressions is a list of string and/or numeric expressions separated by commas or semicolons.

The WRITE# and PRINT# statements differ in that WRITE# inserts commas between the items as they are written and delimits strings with quotation marks, making explicit delimiters in the list unnecessary. Another difference is that WRITE# does not put a blank in front of a positive number. After the last item in the list is written, a carriage return/line feed sequence is inserted.

Examples:

Let A\$ = "CAMERA" and B\$ = "93604-1". The following statement:

```
WRITE#1,A$,B$
```

writes the following image to disk:

```
"CAMERA", "93604-1"
```

A subsequent INPUT\$ statement, such as the following, would input "CAMERA" to A\$ and "93604-1" to B\$:

```
INPUT#1,A$,B$
```

Appendix A
Error Codes and Messages

Code:	Message:

1 `NEXT without FOR`

NEXT statement does not have a corresponding FOR statement. Check variable at FOR statement for a match with the NEXT statement variable.

2 `Syntax error`

A line is encountered that contains an incorrect sequence of characters (such as unmatched parentheses, a misspelled command or statement, incorrect punctuation). This error causes GW-BASIC to display the incorrect line in edit mode.

3 `RETURN without GOSUB`

A RETURN statement is encountered for which there is no previous GOSUB statement.

4 `Out of DATA`

A READ statement is executed when there are no DATA statements with unread data remaining in the program.

5 `Illegal function call`

An out-of-range parameter is passed to a math or string function. An illegal function call error may also occur as the result of

- a negative or unreasonably large subscript
- a negative or zero argument with LOG
- a negative argument to SQR
- a negative mantissa with a noninteger power

- a call to a USR function for which the starting address has not yet been given

- an improper argument to MID\$, LEFT\$, RIGHT\$, INP, OUT, WAIT, PEEK, POKE, TAB, SPC, STRING\$, SPACE\$, INSTR, or ON...GOTO

6   Overflow

The result of a calculation is too large to be represented in GW-BASIC's number format. If underflow occurs, the result is zero, and execution continues without an error.

7   Out of memory

A program is too large, has too many FOR loops, GOSUBs, variables, or expressions that are too complicated. Use the CLEAR statement to set aside more stack space or memory area.

8   Undefined line number

A line reference in a GOTO, GOSUB, IF-THEN...ELSE, or DELETE is a nonexistent line.

9   Subscript out of range

An array element is referenced either with a subscript that is outside the dimensions of the array, or with the wrong number of subscripts.

10   Duplicate Definition

Two DIM statements are given for the same array, or a DIM statement is given for an array after the default dimension of 10 has been established for that array.

11   Division by zero

A division by zero is encountered in an expression, or the operation of involution results in zero being raised to a negative power. Machine infinity with the sign of the numerator is supplied as the result of the division, or positive machine infinity is supplied as the result of the involution, and execution continues.

12   Illegal direct

A statement that is illegal in direct mode is entered as a direct mode command.

13   Type mismatch

A string variable name is assigned a numeric value or vice versa; a function that expects a numeric argument is given a string argument or vice versa.

14   Out of string space

String variables have caused GW-BASIC to exceed the amount of free memory remaining. GW-BASIC allocates string space dynamically until it runs out of memory.

15   String too long

An attempt is made to create a string more than 255 characters long.

16   String formula too complex

A string expression is too long or too complex. Break the expression into smaller expressions.

17   Can't continue

An attempt is made to continue a program that

- has halted because of an error
- has been modified during a break in execution
- does not exist

18   Undefined user function

A USR function is called before the function definition (DEF statement) is given.

19   No RESUME

An error-trapping routine is entered but contains no RESUME statement.

20   RESUME without error

A RESUME statement is encountered before an error-trapping routine is entered.

21   Unprintable error

No error message is available for the existing error condition. This is usually caused by an error with an undefined error code.

22   Missing operand

An expression contains an operator with no operand following it.

23   Line buffer overflow

An attempt is made to input a line that has too many characters.

24   Device Timeout

GW-BASIC did not receive information from an I/O device within a predetermined amount of time.

25   Device Fault

Indicates a hardware error in the printer or interface card.

26   FOR Without NEXT

A FOR was encountered without a matching NEXT.

27   Out of Paper

The printer is out of paper; or, a printer fault.

28   Unprintable error

No error message is available for the existing error condition. This is usually caused by an error with an undefined error code.

29   WHILE without WEND

A WHILE statement does not have a matching WEND.

30   WEND without WHILE

A WEND was encountered without a matching WHILE.

31-49   Unprintable error

No error message is available for the existing error condition. This is usually caused by an error with an undefined error code.

50   FIELD overflow

A FIELD statement is attempting to allocate more bytes than were specified for the record length of a random file.

51   Internal error

An internal malfunction has occurred in GW-BASIC. Report to your dealer the conditions under which the message appeared.

52   Bad file number

A statement or command references a file with a file number that is not open or is out of range of file numbers specified at initialization.

53   File not found

A LOAD, KILL, NAME, FILES, or OPEN statement references a file that does not exist on the current diskette.

54   Bad file mode

An attempt is made to use PUT, GET, or LOF with a sequential file, to LOAD a random file, or to execute an OPEN with a file mode other than I, O, A, or R.

55   File already open

A sequential output mode OPEN is issued for a file that is already open, or a KILL is given for a file that is open.

56   Unprintable error

An error message is not available for the error condition which exists. This is usually caused by an error with an undefined error code.

57   Device I/O Error

Usually a disk I/O error, but generalized to include all I/O devices. It is a fatal error; that is, the operating system cannot recover from the error.

58   File already exists

The filename specified in a NAME statement is identical to a filename already in use on the diskette.

59-60   Unprintable error

No error message is available for the existing error condition. This is usually caused by an error with an undefined error code.

61   Disk full

All disk storage space is in use.

62   Input past end

An INPUT statement is executed after all the data in the file has been input, or for a null (empty) file. To avoid this error, use the EOF function to detect the end of file.

63   Bad record number

In a PUT or GET statement, the record number is either greater than the maximum allowed (16,777,215) or equal to zero.

64   Bad filename

An illegal form is used for the filename with LOAD, SAVE, KILL, or OPEN; for example, a filename with too many characters.

65   Unprintable error

No error message is available for the existing error condition. This is usually caused by an error with an undefined error code.

66   Direct statement in file

A direct statement is encountered while loading a ASCII-format file. The LOAD is terminated.

67   Too many files

An attempt is made to create a new file (using SAVE or OPEN) when all directory entries are full or the file specifications are invalid.

68   Device Unavailable

An attempt is made to open a file to a nonexistent device. It may be that hardware does not exist to support the device, such as **lpt2**: or **lpt3**:, or is disabled by the user. This occurs if an OPEN "COM1: statement is executed but the user disables RS-232 support with the /**c**: switch directive on the command line.

69   Communication buffer overflow

Occurs when a communications input statement is executed, but the input queue is already full. Use an ON ERROR GOTO statement to retry the input when this condition occurs. Subsequent inputs attempt to clear this fault unless characters continue to be received faster than the program can process them. In this case several options are available:

- Increase the size of the COM receive buffer with the /**c**: switch.

- Implement a hand-shaking protocol with the host/satellite (such as: XON/XOFF, as demonstrated in the TTY programming example) to turn transmit off long enough to catch up.

- Use a lower baud rate for transmit and receive.

70   Permission Denied

This is one of three hard disk errors returned from the diskette controller.

- An attempt has been made to write onto a diskette that is write protected.

- Another process has attempted to access a file already in use.

- The UNLOCK range specified does not match the preceding LOCK statement.

71   Disk not Ready

Occurs when the diskette drive door is open or a diskette is
not in the drive. Use an ON ERROR GOTO statement to
recover.

72   Disk media error

Occurs when the diskette controller detects a hardware or
media fault. This usually indicates damaged media. Copy
any existing files to a new diskette and reformat the damaged diskette. FORMAT maps the bad tracks in the file allo-
cation table. The remainder of the diskette is now usable.

73   Advanced Feature

An attempt was made to use a reserved word that is not
available in this version of GW-BASIC.

74   Rename across disks

Occurs when an attempt is made to rename a file to a new
name declared to be on a disk other than the disk specified
for the old name. The naming operation is not performed.

75   Path/File Access Error

During an OPEN, MKDIR, CHDIR, or RMDIR operation,
MS-DOS is unable to make a correct path-to-filename connection. The operation is not completed.

76   Path not found

During an OPEN, MKDIR, CHDIR, or RMDIR operation,
MS-DOS is unable to find the path specified. The operation
is not completed.

Appendix B
Mathematical Functions

Mathematical functions not intrinsic to GW-BASIC can be calculated as follows:

Function	GW-BASIC Equivalent
Secant	SEC(X) = 1/COS(X)
Cosecant	CSC(X) = 1/SIN(X)
Cotangent	COT(X) = 1/TAN(X)
Inverse Sine	ARCSIN(X) = ATN(X/SQR(-X*X + 1))
Inverse Cosine	ARCCOS(X) = ATN (X/SQR(-X*X + 1)) + $\pi/2$
Inverse Secant	ARCSEC(X) = ATN(X/SQR(X*X-1)) + SGN(SGN(X)-1)* $\pi/2$
Inverse Cosecant	ARCCSC(X) = ATN(X/SQR(X*X-1)) + SGN(X)-1)* $\pi/2$
Inverse Cotangent	ARCCOT(X) = ATN(X) + $\pi/2$
Hyperbolic Sine	SINH(X) = (EXP(X)-EXP(-X))/2
Hyperbolic Cosine	COSH(X) = (EXP(X) + EXP(-X))/2
Hyperbolic Tangent	TANH(X) = (EXP(X)-EXP(-X))/(EXP(X) + EXP(-X))
Hyperbolic Secant	SECH(X) = 2/(EXP(X) + EXP(-X))
Hyperbolic Cosecant	CSCH(X) = 2/(EXP(X)-EXP(-X))
Hyperbolic Cotangent	COTH(X) = EXP(-X)/(EXP(X)-EXP(-X))*2 + 1

Inverse Hyperbolic Sine	ARCSINH(X) = LOG(X/SQR(X*X + 1))
Inverse Hyperbolic Cosine	ARCCOSH(X) = LOG(X + SQR(X*X-1))
Inverse Hyperbolic Tangent	ARCTANH(X) = LOG((1 + X)/(1-X))/2
Inverse Hyperbolic Cosecant	ARCCSCH(X) = LOG(SGN(X)*SQR(X*X + 1) + 1)/X
Inverse Hyperbolic Secant	ARCSECH(X) = LOG(SQR(-X*X + 1) + 1)/X
Inverse Hyperbolic Cotangent	ARCCOTH(X) = LOG((X + 1)/(X-1))/2

Appendix C
ASCII Character Codes

Dec	Oct	Hex	Chr	Dec	Oct	Hex	Chr
000	000	00H	NUL	032	040	20H	SP
001	001	01H	SOH	033	041	21H	!
002	002	02H	STX	034	042	22H	"
003	003	03H	ETX	035	043	23H	#
004	004	04H	EOT	036	044	24H	$
005	005	05H	ENQ	037	045	25H	%
006	006	06H	ACK	038	046	26H	&
007	007	07H	BEL	039	047	27H	'
008	010	08H	BS	040	050	28H	(
009	011	09H	HT	041	051	29H	)
010	012	0AH	LF	042	052	2AH	*
011	013	0BH	VT	043	053	2BH	+
012	014	0CH	FF	044	054	2CH	,
013	015	0DH	CR	045	055	2DH	-
014	016	0EH	SO	046	056	2EH	.
015	017	0FH	SI	047	057	2FH	/
016	020	10H	DLE	048	060	30H	0
017	021	11H	DC1	049	061	31H	1
018	022	12H	DC2	050	062	32H	2
019	023	13H	DC3	051	063	33H	3
020	024	14H	DC4	052	064	34H	4
021	025	15H	NAK	053	065	35H	5
022	026	16H	SYN	054	066	36H	6
023	027	17H	ETB	055	067	37H	7
024	030	18H	CAN	056	070	38H	8
025	031	19H	EM	057	071	39H	9
026	032	1AH	SUB	058	072	3AH	:
027	033	1BH	ESC	059	073	3BH	;
028	034	1CH	FS	060	074	3CH	<
029	035	1DH	GS	061	075	3DH	=
030	036	1EH	RS	062	076	3EH	>
031	037	1FH	US	063	077	3FH	?

Dec = Decimal, Oct = Octal, Hex = Hexadecimal(H), Chr = Character, LF = Line feed
FF = Form feed, CR = Carriage return, DEL = Rubout

Appendix C *(continued)*

Dec	Oct	Hex	Chr	Dec	Oct	Hex	Chr
064	100	40H	@	096	140	60H	`
065	101	41H	A	097	141	61H	a
066	102	42H	B	098	142	62H	b
067	103	43H	C	099	143	63H	c
068	104	44H	D	100	144	64H	d
069	105	45H	E	101	145	65H	e
070	106	46H	F	102	146	66H	f
071	107	47H	G	103	147	67H	g
072	110	48H	H	104	150	68H	h
073	111	49H	I	105	151	69H	i
074	112	4AH	J	106	152	6AH	j
075	113	4BH	K	107	153	6BH	k
076	114	4CH	L	108	154	6CH	l
077	115	4DH	M	109	155	6DH	m
078	116	4EH	N	110	156	6EH	n
079	117	4FH	O	111	157	6FH	o
080	120	50H	P	112	160	70H	p
081	121	51H	Q	113	161	71H	q
082	122	52H	R	114	162	72H	r
083	123	53H	S	115	163	73H	s
084	124	54H	T	116	164	74H	t
085	125	55H	U	117	165	75H	u
086	126	56H	V	118	166	76H	v
087	127	57H	W	119	167	77H	w
088	130	58H	X	120	170	78H	x
089	131	59H	Y	121	171	79H	y
090	132	5AH	Z	122	172	7AH	z
091	133	5BH	[	123	173	7BH	{
092	134	5CH	\	124	174	7CH		
093	135	5DH	]	125	175	7DH	}
094	136	5EH	^	126	176	7EH	~
095	137	5FH	–	127	177	7FH	DEL

Dec = Decimal, Oct = Octal, Hex = Hexadecimal(H), Chr = Character, LF = Line feed
FF = Form feed, CR = Carriage return, DEL = Rubout

Appendix D

Assembly Language (Machine Code) Subroutines

This appendix is written primarily for users experienced in assembly language programming.

GW-BASIC lets you interface with assembly language subroutines by using the USR function and the CALL statement.

The USR function allows assembly language subroutines to be called in the same way GW-BASIC intrinsic functions are called. However, the CALL statement is recommended for interfacing machine language programs with GW-BASIC. The CALL statement is compatible with more languages than the USR function call, produces more readable source code, and can pass multiple arguments.

D.1 Memory Allocation

Memory space must be set aside for an assembly language (or machine code) subroutine before it can be loaded. There are three recommended ways to set aside space for assembly language routines:

- Specify an array and use VARPTR to locate the start of the array before every access.

- Use the /m switch in the command line. Get GW-BASIC's Data segment (DS), and add the size of DS to reference the reserved space above the data segment.

- Execute a .COM file that stays resident, and store a pointer to it in an unused interrupt vector location.

There are three recommended ways to load assembly language routines:

- BLOAD the file. Use DEBUG to load in an .EXE file that is in high memory, run GW-BASIC, and BSAVE the .EXE file.

- Execute a .COM file that contains the routines. Save the pointer to these routines in unused interrupt-vector locations, so that your application in GW-BASIC can get the pointer and use the routine(s).

- Place the routine into the specified area.

If, when an assembly language subroutine is called, more stack space is needed, GW-BASIC stack space can be saved, and a new stack set up for use by the assembly language subroutine. The GW-BASIC stack space must be restored, however, before returning from the subroutine.

D.2   CALL Statement

CALL *variablename*[(*arguments*)]

variablename contains the offset in the current segment of the subroutine being called.

arguments are the variables or constants, separated by commas, that are to be passed to the routine.

For each parameter in *arguments*, the 2-byte offset of the parameter's location within the data segment (DS) is pushed onto the stack.

The GW-BASIC return address code segment (CS), and offset (IP) are pushed onto the stack.

A long call to the segment address given in the last DEF SEG statement and the offset given in *variablename* transfers control to the user's routine.

The stack segment (SS), data segment (DS), extra segment (ES), and the stack pointer (SP) must be preserved.

Figure D.1 shows the state of the stack at the time of the CALL statement:

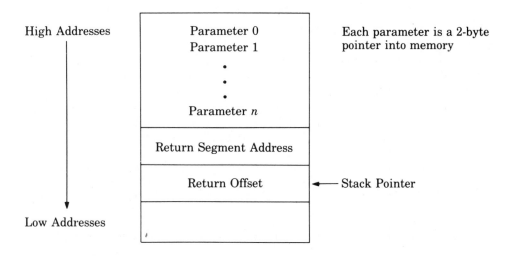

Figure D.1 Stack Layout When the CALL Statement is Activated

The user's routine now has control. Parameters may be referenced by moving the stack pointer (SP) to the base pointer (BP) and adding a positive offset to BP.

Upon entry, the segment registers DS, ES, and SS all point to the address of the segment that contains the GW-BASIC interpreter code. The code segment register CS contains the latest value supplied by DEF SEG. If no DEF SEG has been specified, it then points to the same address as DS, ES, and SS (the default DEF SEG).

Figure D.2 shows the condition of the stack during execution of the called subroutine:

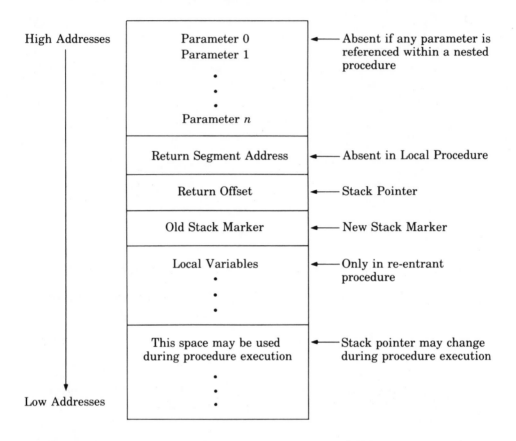

Figure D.2 Stack Layout During Execution of a CALL Statement

The following seven rules must be observed when coding a subroutine:

1. The called routine may destroy the contents of the AX, BX, CX, DX, SI, DI, and BP registers. They do not require restoration upon return to GW-BASIC. However, all segment registers and the stack pointer must be restored. Good programming practice dictates that interrupts enabled or disabled be restored to the state observed upon entry.

2. The called program must know the number and length of the parameters passed. References to parameters are positive offsets added to BP, assuming the called routine moved the current stack pointer into BP; that is, MOV BP,SP. When 3 parameters are passed, the location of PO is at BP + 10, P1 is at BP + 8, and P2 is at BP + 6.

3. The called routine must do a RETURN *n* (*n* is two times the number of parameters in the argument list) to adjust the stack to the start of the calling sequence. Also, programs must be defined by a PROC FAR statement.

4. Values are returned to GW-BASIC by including in the argument list the variable name that receives the result.

5. If the argument is a string, the parameter offset points to three bytes called the *string descriptor*. Byte 0 of the string descriptor contains the length of the string (0 to 255). Bytes 1 and 2, respectively, are the lower and upper eight bits of the string starting address in string space.

Note

The called routine must not change the contents of any of the three bytes of the string descriptor.

---

6. Strings may be altered by user routines, but their length must not be changed. GW-BASIC cannot correctly manipulate strings if their lengths are modified by external routines.

7. If the argument is a string literal in the program, the string descriptor points to program text. Be careful not to alter or destroy your program this way. To avoid unpredictable results, add + "" to the string literal in the program. For example, the following line forces the string literal to be copied into string space allocated outside of program memory space:

```
20 A$="BASIC"+""
```

The string can then be modified without affecting the program.

Examples:

```
100 DEF SEG=&H2000
110 ACC=&H7FA
```

```
120 CALL ACC(A,B$,C)
    .
    .
    .
```

Line 100 sets the segment to 2000 hex. The value of variable ACC is added into the address as the low word after the DEF SEG value is left-shifted four bits (this is a function of the microprocessor, not of GW-BASIC). Here, ACC is set to &H7FA, so that the call to ACC executes the subroutine at location 2000:7FA hex.

Upon entry, only 16 bytes (eight words) remain available within the allocated stack space. If the called program requires additional stack space, then the user program must reset the stack pointer to a new allocated space. Be sure to restore the stack pointer adjusted to the start of the calling sequence on return to GW-BASIC.

The following assembly language sequence demonstrates access of the parameters passed and storage of a return result in the variable C.

Note

The called program must know the variable type for numeric parameters passed. In these examples, the following instruction copies only two bytes:

```
MOVSW
```

This is adequate if variables A and C are integer. It would be necessary to copy four bytes if they were single precision, or copy eight bytes if they were double precision.

```
MOV BP,SP          Gets the current stack position in BP
MOV BX,8[BP]       Gets the address of B$ description
MOV CL,[BX]        Gets the length of B$ in CL
MOV DX,1[BX]       Gets the address of B$ string descriptor in DX
MOV SI,10[BP]      Gets the address of A in SI
MOV DI,6[BP]       Gets the pointer to C in DI
MOVSW              Stores variable A in 'C'
RET 6              Restores stack; returns
```

D.3   USR Function Calls

Although the CALL statement is the recommended way of calling assembly language subroutines, the USR function call is still available for compatibility with previously-written programs.

Syntax:

USR[*n*](*argument*)

n is a number from 0 to 9 which specifies the USR routine being called (see DEF USR statement). If *n* is omitted, USR0 is assumed.

argument is any numeric or string expression.

In GW-BASIC a DEF SEG statement should be executed prior to a USR function call to ensure that the code segment points to the subroutine being called. The segment address given in the DEF SEG statement determines the starting segment of the subroutine.

For each USR function call, a corresponding DEF USR statement must have been executed to define the USR function call offset. This offset and the currently active DEF SEG address determine the starting address of the subroutine.

When the USR function call is made, register AL contains the *number type flag* (NTF), which specifies the type of argument given. The NTF value may be one of the following:

NTF Value	Specifies
2	a two-byte integer (two's complement format)
3	a string
4	a single-precision floating-point number
8	a double-precision floating-point number

If the argument of a USR function call is a number (AL<>73), the value of the argument is placed in the *floating-point accumulator* (FAC). The FAC is 8 bytes long and is in the GW-BASIC data segment. Register BX will point at the fifth byte of the FAC. Figure D.3 shows the representation of all the GW-BASIC number types in the FAC:

				least significant byte	most significant byte					Integer

				least significant byte			most significant byte	exponent minus 128		Single Precision

sign byte

least significant byte							most significant byte	exponent minus 128		Double Precision

sign byte

Figure D.3 Number Types in the Floating-Point Accumulator

If the argument is a single-precision floating-point number:

- BX + 3 is the exponent, minus 128. The binary point is to the left of the most significant bit of the mantissa.

- BX + 2 contains the highest seven bits of mantissa with leading 1 suppressed (implied). Bit 7 is the sign of the number (0 = positive, 1 = negative).

- BX + 1 contains the middle 8 bits of the mantissa.

- BX + 0 contains the lowest 8 bits of the mantissa.

If the argument is an integer:

- BX + 1 contains the upper eight bits of the argument.

- BX + 0 contains the lower eight bits of the argument.

If the argument is a double-precision floating-point number:

- BX + 0 through BX + 3 are the same as for single-precision floating point.

- BX-1 to BX-4 contain four more bytes of mantissa. BX-4 contains the lowest eight bits of the mantissa.

If the argument is a string (indicated by the value 3 stored in the AL register) the (DX) register pair points to three bytes called the string descriptor. Byte 0 of the string descriptor contains the length of the string (0 to 255). Bytes 1 and 2, respectively, are the lower- and upper-eight bits of the string starting address in the GW-BASIC data segment.

If the argument is a string literal in the program, the string descriptor points to program text. Be careful not to alter or destroy programs this way (see the preceding CALL statement).

Usually, the value returned by a USR function call is the same type (integer, string, single precision, or double precision) as the argument that was passed to it. The registers that must be preserved are the same as in the CALL statement.

A far return is required to exit the USR subroutine. The returned value must be stored in the FAC.

D.4   Programs That Call Assembly Language Programs

This section contains two sample GW-BASIC programs that

- load an assembly language routine to add two numbers together
- return the sum into memory
- remain resident in memory

The code segment and offset to the first routine is stored in interrupt vector at 0:100H.

Example 1 calls an assembly language subroutine:

Example 1

```
10 DEF SEG=0
100 CS=PEEK(&H102)+PEEK(&H103)*256
200 OFFSET=PEEK(&H100)+PEEK(&H101)*256
250 DEF SEG
```

```
300 C1%=2:C2%=3:C3%=0
400 TWOSUM=OFFSET
500 DEF SEG=CS
600 CALL TWOSUM(C1%,C2%,C3%)
700 PRINT C3%
800 END
```

The assembly language subroutine called in the above program must be
assembled, linked, and converted to a .COM file. The program, when executed prior to the running of the GW-BASIC program, will remain in memory
until the system power is turned off, or the system is rebooted.

```
0100                     org 100H
0100                     double    segment
                         assume  cs:double
0100    EB 17 90    start:          jmp      start1
0103                     usrprg   proc far
0103    55               push bp
0104    8B EC            mov bp,sp
0106    8B 76 08         mov si,[bp]+8          ;get address of
                                                ;parameter b
0109    8B 04            mov ax,[si]            ;get value of b
010B    8B 76 0A         mov si,[bp]+10         ;get address of
                                                ;parameter a
010E    03 04            add ax,[si]            ;add value of
                                                ;a to value of
                                                ;b
0110    8B 7E 06         mov di,[bp]+6          ;get address of
                                                ;parameter c
0113    89 05            mov di,ax              ;store sum in
                                                ;parameter c

0115    5D               pop bp
0116    ca 0006          ret 6
0119                     usrprg endp

                                                ;
                                                ;Program to put
                                                ;procedure in memory
                                                ;and remain resident.
                                                ;The offset and
                                                ;segment are stored
                                                ;in location 100-103H.
0119                     start1:
0119    B8 0000          mov ax,0
011C    8E D8            mov ds,ax              ;data segment to 0000H
011E    BB 0100          mov bx,0100H           ;pointer to int vector
                                                ;100H
0121    83 7F 02 0  cmp word ptr [bx],0
0125    75 16            jne quit               ;program
                                                ;already run, exit
```

```
0127        83 3F 00      cmp word ptr2 [bx],0
012A        75 11         jne quit              ;program
                                                ;already run,
                                                ;exit
012C        B8 0103 R     mov ax,offset usrprg
012F        89 07         mov [bx],ax           ;program offset
0131        8C c8         mov ax,cs
0133        89 47 02      mov [bx+2],ax         ;data segment
0136        0E            push cs
0137        1F            pop ds
0138        BA 0141 R     mov dx,offset veryend
013B        CD 27         int 27h
013D                  quit:
013D        CD 20          int 20h
013F                  veryend:
013F                  double ends
                      end start
```

Example 2 places the assembly language subroutine in the specified area:

Example 2

```
10   I=0:JC=0
100  DIM A%(23)
150  MEM%=VARPTR(A%(1))
200  FOR I=1 TO 23
300  READ JC
400  POKE MEM%,JC
450  MEM%=MEM%+1
500  NEXT
600  C1%=2:C2%=3:C3%=0
700  TWOSUM=VARPTR(A%(1))
800  CALL TWOSUM(C1%,C2%,C3%)
900  PRINT C3%
950  END
1000 DATA &H55,&H8b,&Hec &H8b,&H76,&H08,&H8b,&H04,&H8b,&H76
1100 DATA &H0a,&H03,&H04,&H8b,&H7e,&H06,&H89,&H05,&H5d
1200 DATA &Hca,&H06,&H00
```

Appendix E
Converting BASIC Programs to GW-BASIC

Programs written in a BASIC language other than GW-BASIC may require some minor adjustments before they can be run. The following sections describe these adjustments.

E.1   String Dimensions

Delete all statements used to declare the length of strings. A statement such as the following:

```
DIM A$(I,J)
```

which dimensions a string array for J elements of length I, should be converted to the following statement:

```
DIM A$(J)
```

Some GW-BASIC languages use a comma or ampersand (&) for string concatenation. Each of these must be changed to a plus sign (+), which is the operator for GW-BASIC string concatenation.

In GW-BASIC, the MID$, RIGHT$, and LEFT$ functions are used to take substrings of strings. Forms such as A$(I) to access the Ith character in A$, or A$(I,J) to take a substring of A$ from position I to position J, must be changed as follows:

Other BASIC:	GW-BASIC:
X$ = A$(I)	X$ = MID$(A$,I,1)
X$ = A$(I,J)	X$ = MID$(A$,I,J-I+1)

If the substring reference is on the left side of an assignment, and X$ is used to replace characters in A$, convert as follows:

Other BASIC:	GW-BASIC:
A$(I) = X$	MID$(A$,I,1) = X$
A$(I,J) = X$	MID$(A$,I,J-I + 1) = X$

E.2   Multiple Assignments

Some GW-BASIC languages allow statements of the following form to set B and C equal to zero:

```
10 LET B=C=0
```

GW-BASIC would interpret the second equal sign as a logical operator and set B equal to -1 if C equaled 0. Convert this statement to two assignment statements:

```
10 C=0:B=0
```

E.3   Multiple Statements

Some GW-BASIC languages use a backslash ($\backslash$) to separate multiple statements on a line. With GW-BASIC, be sure all elements on a line are separated by a colon (:).

E.4   MAT Functions

Programs using the MAT functions available in some GW-BASIC languages must be rewritten using FOR-NEXT loops to execute properly.

E.5 FOR-NEXT Loops

Some GW-BASIC languages will always execute a FOR-NEXT loop once, regardless of the limits. GW-BASIC checks the limits first and does not execute the loop if past limits.

Appendix F
Communications

This appendix describes the GW-BASIC statements necessary to support RS-232 asynchronous communications with other computers and peripheral devices.

F.1   Opening Communications Files

The OPEN COM statement allocates a buffer for input and output in the same manner as the OPEN statement opens disk files.

F.2   Communications I/O

Since the communications port is opened as a file, all I/O statements valid for disk files are valid for COM.

COM sequential input statements are the same as those for disk files:

INPUT#
LINE INPUT#
INPUT$

COM sequential output statements are the same as those for diskette:

PRINT#
PRINT# USING

See the *GW-BASIC User's Reference* for more information on these statements.

F.3   The COM I/O Functions

The most difficult aspect of asynchronous communications is processing characters as quickly as they are received. At rates above 2400 baud (bps), it is necessary to suspend character transmission from the host long enough for the receiver to catch up. This can be done by sending XOFF (CTRL-S) to the host to temporarily suspend transmission, and XON (CTRL-Q) to resume, if the application supports it.

GW-BASIC provides three functions which help to determine when an over-run condition is imminent:

LOC(x)   Returns the number of characters in the input queue waiting to be read. The input queue can hold more than 255 characters (determined by the /c: switch). If there are more than 255 characters in the queue, LOC(x) returns 255. Since a string is limited to 255 characters, this practical limit alleviates the need for the programmer to test for string size before reading data into it.

LOF(x)   Returns the amount of free space in the input queue; that is

/c:*(size)-number of characters in the input queue*

LOF may be used to detect when the input queue is reaching storage capacity.

EOF(x)   True (−1), indicates that the input queue is empty. False (0) is returned if any characters are waiting to be read.

F.4   Possible Errors:

A "Communications buffer overflow" error occurs if a read is attempted after the input queue is full (that is, LOC(x) returns 0).

A "Device I/O" error occurs if any of the following line conditions are detected on receive: overrun error (OE), framing error (FE), or break interrupt (BI). The error is reset by subsequent inputs, but the character causing the error is lost.

A "Device fault" error occurs if data set ready (DSR) is lost during I/O.

A "Parity error" occurs if the PE (parity enable) option was used in the OPEN COM statement and incorrect parity was received.

F.5   The INPUT$ Function

The INPUT$ function is preferred over the INPUT and LINE INPUT statements for reading COM files, because all ASCII characters may be significant in communications. INPUT is least desirable because input stops when a comma or an enter is seen. LINE INPUT terminates when an enter is seen.

INPUT$ allows all characters read to be assigned to a string.

INPUT$ returns x characters from the y file. The following statements then are most efficient for reading a COM file:

```
10  WHILE NOT EOF(1)
20  A$=INPUT$(LOC(1),#1)
30  ...
40  ... Process data returned in A$ ...
50  ...
60  WEND
```

This sequence of statements translates: As long as something is in the input queue, return the number of characters in the queue and store them in A$. If there are more than 255 characters, only 255 are returned at a time to prevent string overflow. If this is the case, EOF(1) is false, and input continues until the input queue is empty.

GET and PUT Statements for COM Files

Purpose:

To allow fixed-length I/O for COM.

Syntax:

GET *filenumber, nbytes* **PUT** *filenumber, nbytes*

Comments:

filenumber is an integer expression returning a valid file number.

nbytes is an integer expression returning the number of bytes to be transferred into or out of the file buffer. *nbytes* cannot exceed the value set by the /s: switch when GW-BASIC was invoked.

Because of the low performance associated with telephone line communications, it is recommended that GET and PUT not be used in such applications.

Example:

The following TTY sample program is an exercise in communications I/O. It is designed to enable your computer to be used as a conventional terminal. Besides full-duplex communications with a host, the TTY program allows data to be downloaded to a file. Conversely, a file may be uploaded (transmitted) to another machine.

In addition to demonstrating the elements of asynchronous communications, this program is useful for transferring GW-BASIC programs and data to and from a computer.

Note

> This program is set up to communicate with a DEC® SYSTEM-20 especially in the use of XON and XOFF. It may require modification to communicate with other types of hardware.

F.6   The TTY Sample Program

```
10 SCREEN 0,0:WIDTH 80
15 KEY OFF:CLS:CLOSE
20 DEFINT A-Z
25 LOCATE 25,1
30 PRINT STRING$(60," ")
40 FALSE=0:TRUE=NOT FALSE
50 MENU=5 'Value of MENU Key (^E)
60 XOFF$=CHR$(19):XON$=CHR$(17)
100 LOCATE 25,1:PRINT "Async TTY Program";
110 LOCATE 1,1:LINE INPUT "Speed?";"SPEED$
120 COMFIL$="COM1:,+SPEED$+",E,7"
130 OPEN COMFIL$ AS #1
140 OPEN "SCRN:"FOR OUTPUT AS #3
200 PAUSE=FALSE
210 A$=INKEY$:IF A$=""THEN 230
220 IF ASC(A$)=MENU THEN 300 ELSE PRINT #1,A$;
230 IF EOF(1) THEN 210
240 IF LOC(1)>128 THEN PAUSE=TRUE:PRINT #1,XOFF$;
250 A$=INPUT$(LOC(1),#1)
260 PRINT #3,A$;:IF LOC(1)>0 THEN 240
270 IF PAUSE THEN PAUSE=FALSE:PRINT #1,XON$;
280 GOTO 210
300 LOCATE 1,1:PRINT STRING$(30,32):LOCATE 1,1
310 LINE INPUT "FILE?";DSKFIL$
400 LOCATE 1,1:PRINT STRING$(30,32):LOCATE 1,1
410 LINE INPUT"(T)ransmit or (R)eceive?";TXRX$
420 IF TXRX$="T" THEN OPEN DSKFIL$ FOR INPUT AS #2:GOTO 1000
430 OPEN DSKFIL$ FOR OUTPUT AS #2
440 PRINT #1,CHR$(13);
500 IF EOF(1) THEN GOSUB 600
510 IF LOC(1)>128 THEN PAUSE=TRUE:PRINT #1,XOFF$;
520 A$=INPUT$(LOC(1),#1)
530 PRINT #2,A$;:IF LOC(1)>0 THEN 510
540 IF PAUSE THEN PAUSE=FALSE:PRINT #1,XON$;
550 GOTO 500
600 FOR I=1 TO 5000
610 IF NOT EOF(1) THEN I=9999
620 NEXT I
630 IF I>9999 THEN RETURN
640 CLOSE #2;CLS:LOCATE 25,10:PRINT "* Download complete *";
650 RETURN 200
1000 WHILE NOT EOF(2)
1010 A$=INPUT$(1,#2)
1020 PRINT #1,A$;
1030 WEND
1040 PRINT #1,CHR$(28);^Z to make close file.
```

```
1050 CLOSE #2:CLS:LOCATE 25,10:PRINT "** Upload complete **";
1060 GOTO 200
9999 CLOSE:KEY ON
```

F.7   Notes on the TTY Sample Program

Note

Asynchronous implies character I/O as opposed to line or block I/O. Therefore, all prints (either to the COM file or screen) are terminated with a semicolon (;). This retards the return line feed normally issued at the end of the PRINT statement.

Line Number	Comments
10	Sets the SCREEN to black and white alpha mode and sets the width to 80.
15	Turns off the soft key display, clears the screen, and makes sure that all files are closed.
20	Defines all numeric variables as integer, primarily for the benefit of the subroutine at 600-620. Any program looking for speed optimization should use integer counters in loops where possible.
40	Defines boolean true and false.
50	Defines the ASCII (ASC) value of the MENU key.
60	Defines the ASCII XON and XOFF characters.
100-130	Prints program ID and asks for baud rate (speed). Opens communications to file number 1, even parity, 7 data bits.
200-280	This section performs full-duplex I/O between the video screen and the device connected to the RS-232 connector as follows:

1. Read a character from the keyboard into A$. INKEY$ returns a null string if no character is waiting.

2. If a keyboard character is available, waiting, then:

   If the character is the MENU key, the operator is ready to down-load a file. Get filename.

   If the character (A$) is not the MENU key, send it by writing to the communications file (PRINT #1...).

3. If no character is waiting, check to see if any characters are being received.

4. At 230, see if any characters are waiting in COM buffer. If not, go back and check the keyboard.

5. At 240, if more than 128 characters are waiting, set PAUSE flag to indicate that input is being suspended. Send XOFF to host, stopping further transmission.

6. At 250-260, read and display contents of COM buffer on screen until empty. Continue to monitor size of COM buffer (in 240). Suspend transmission if reception falls behind.

7. Resume host transmission by sending XON only if suspended by previous XOFF.

8. Repeat process until the MENU key is pressed.

300-320	Get disk filename to be down-loaded to. Open the file as number 2.
400-420	Asks if file named is to be transmitted (up-loaded) or received (down-loaded).
430	Receive routine. Sends a RETURN to the host to begin the down-load. This program assumes that the last command sent to the host was to begin such a transfer and was missing only the terminating return. If a DEC system is the host, such a command might be

COPY TTY:=MANUAL.MEM (MENU Key)

if the MENU key was struck instead of RETURN.

500	When no more characters are being received, (LOC(x) returns 0), the program performs a timeout routine.
510	If more than 128 characters are waiting, signal a pause and send XOFF to the host.
520-530	Read all characters in COM queue (LOC(x)) and write them to diskette (PRINT #2...) until reception is caught up to transmission.
540-550	If a pause is issued, restart host by sending XON and clearing the pause flag. Continue the process until no characters are received for a predetermined time.
600-650	Time-out subroutine. The FOR loop count was determined by experimentation. If no character is received from the host for 17-20 seconds, transmission is assumed complete. If any character is received during this time (line 610), then set n well above the FOR loop range to exit loop and return to caller. If host transmission is complete, close the disk file and resume regular activities.
1000-1060	Transmit routine. Until end of disk file, read one character into A$ with INPUT$ statement. Send character to COM device in 1020. Send a ^Z at end of file in 1040 in case receiving device needs one to close its file. Lines 1050 and 1060 close disk file, print completion message, and go back to conversation mode in line 200.
9999	Presently not executed. As an exercise, add some lines to the routine 400-420 to exit the program via line 9999. This line closes the COM file left open and restores the function key display.

Appendix G
Hexadecimal Equivalents

Table G.1 lists decimal and binary equivalents to hexadecimal values.

Table G.1

**Decimal and Binary Equivalents
to Hexadecimal Values**

Hexadecimal Value	Equals Decimal:	Equals Binary:
0	0	0000
1	1	0001
2	2	0010
3	3	0011
4	4	0100
5	5	0101
6	6	0110
7	7	0111
8	8	1000
9	9	1001
A	10	1010
B	11	1011
C	12	1100
D	13	1101
E	14	1110
F	15	1111

Table G.2 lists decimal equivalents to hexadecimal values.

Table G.2

Decimal Equivalents to Hexadecimal Values

Hexadecimal Value	Equals Decimal:	Hexadecimal Value:	Equals Decimal:
0	0	80	128
1	1	.	
2	2	.	
3	3	.	
4	4	90	144
5	5	.	
6	6	.	
7	7	.	
8	8	A0	160
9	9	.	
A	10	.	
B	11	.	
C	12	B0	176
D	13	.	
E	14	.	
F	15	.	
10	16	C0	192
11	17	.	
12	18	.	
13	19	.	
14	20	D0	208
15	21	.	
16	22	.	
17	23	.	
18	24	E0	224
19	25	.	
1A	26	.	
1B	27	.	
1C	28	F0	240
1D	29	100	256
1E	30	200	512
1F	31	300	768
20	32	400	1024
.	.	500	1280
.	.	600	1536
.	.	700	1792

Table G.2 *(continued)*

Hexadecimal Value	Equals Decimal:	Hexadecimal Value:	Equals Decimal:
30	48	800	2048
.	.	900	2304
.	.	A00	2560
.	.	B00	2816
40	64	C00	3072
.	.	D00	3328
.	.	E00	3584
.	.	F00	3840
50	80	1000	4096
.	.	2000	8192
.	.	3000	12288
.	.	4000	16384
60	96	5000	20480
.	.	6000	24576
.	.	7000	28672
.	.	8000	32768
70	112	9000	36864
.	.	A000	40960
.	.	B000	45056
.	.	C000	49152
		D000	53248
		E000	57344
		F000	61440

Appendix H
Key Scan Codes

Keytop Legend	Scancode
ESC	01
1/!	02
2/@	03
3/#	04
	05
5/%	06
6/^	07
7/&	08
8/*	09
9/(	0A
0/)	0B
-/_	0C
=/+	0D
BACKSPACE	0E
TAB	0F
Q	10
W	11
E	12
R	13
T	14
Y	15
U	16
I	17
O	18
P	19
[/{	1A
]/}	1B
ENTER	1C
CTRL	1D
A	1E
S	1F
D	20
F	21
G	22
H	23
J	24

Keytop Legend	Scancode
K	25
L	26
;/:	27
'/"	28
'/~	29
Left SHIFT	2A
/|	2B
Z	2C
X	2D
C	2E
V	2F
B	30
N	31
M	32
,/<	33
//?	35
Right SHIFT	36
*/PRTSC	37
ALT	38
SPACEBAR	39
CAPS LOCK	3A
F1	3B
F2	3C
F3	3D
F4	3E
F5	3F
F6	40
F7	41
F8	42
F9	43
F10	44
NUM LOCK	45
SCROLL LOCK	46
7/HOME	47
8/CURSOR UP	48
9/PGUP	49

Keytop Legend	Scancode
-	4A
4/CURSOR LEFT	4B
5	4C
6/CURSOR RIGHT	4D
+	4E
1/END	4F
2/CURSOR DOWN	50
3/PGDN	51
0/INS	52
./DEL	53

Appendix I
Characters Recognized by GW-BASIC

The GW-BASIC character set includes all characters that are legal in GW-BASIC commands, statements, functions, and variables. The set comprises alphabetic, numeric, and special characters.

The alphabetic characters in GW-BASIC are the uppercase and lowercase letters of the alphabet.

The numeric characters in GW-BASIC are the digits 0 through 9.

The following special characters and terminal keys are recognized by GW-BASIC:

Character	Description
	Blank.
=	Equal sign or assignment symbol.
+	Plus sign or string concatenation.
-	Minus sign.
*	Asterisk or multiplication symbol.
/	Slash or division symbol.
^	Caret, exponentiation symbol, or CTRL key.
(	Left parenthesis.
)	Right parenthesis.
%	Percent or integer declaration.
#	Number sign or double-precision declaration.
$	Dollar sign or string declaration.
!	Exclamation point or single-precision declaration.

[	Left bracket.
]	Right bracket.
,	Comma.
""	Double quotation marks or string delimiter.
.	Period, dot, or decimal point.
'	Single quotation mark, apostrophe, or remark indicator.
;	Semicolon or carriage return suppressor.
:	Colon or line statement delimiter.
&	Ampersand or descriptor for hexadecimal and octal number conversion.
?	Question mark.
<	Less than symbol.
>	Greater than symbol.
\	Backslash or integer division symbol.
@	"At" sign.
_	Underscore.
BACKSPACE	Deletes last character typed.
ESC	Erases the current logical line from the screen.
TAB	Moves print position to next tab stop. Tab stops are every eight columns.
CURSOR	Moves cursor to next physical line.
RETURN	Terminates input to a line and moves cursor to beginning of the next line, or executes statement in direct mode.

Glossary

abend

An acronym for *abnormal end of task*. An abend is the termination of computer processing on a job or task prior to its completion because of an error condition that cannot be resolved by programmed recovery procedures.

access

The process of seeking, reading, or writing data on a storage unit.

access methods

Techniques and programs used to move data between main memory and input/output devices.

accuracy

The degree of freedom from error. Accuracy is often confused with *precision*, which refers to the degree of preciseness of a measurement.

acronym

A word formed by the initial letters of words or by initial letters plus parts of several words. Acronyms are widely used in computer technology. For example, *COBOL* is an acronym for COmmon Business Oriented Language.

active partition

A section of the computer's memory that houses the *operating system* being used.

address

A name, label, or number identifying a register, location or unit where information is stored.

algebraic language

A language whose statements are structured to resemble the structure of algebraic expression. Fortran is a good example of an algebraic language.

algorithm

A set of well-defined rules or procedures to be followed in order to obtain the solution of a problem in a finite number of steps. An algorithm can involve arithmetic, algebraic, logical and other types of procedures and instructions. An algorithm can be simple or complex. However, all algorithms must produce a solution within a finite number of steps. Algorithms are fundamental when using a computer to solve problems, because the computer must be supplied with a specific set of instructions that yields a solution in a reasonable length of time.

alphabetic

Data representation by alphabetical characters in contrast to numerical; the letters of the alphabet.

alphanumeric

A contraction of the words alphabetic and numeric; a set of characters including letters, numerals, and special symbols.

application

The system or problem to which a computer is applied. Reference is often made to an application as being either of the *computational type*, in which arithmetic computations predominate, or of the *data processing type*, in which data handling operations predominate.

application program

A computer program designed to meet specific user needs.

argument

1. A type of variable whose value is not a direct function of another variable. It can represent the location of a number in a mathematical operation, or the number with which a function works to produce its results.

2. A known reference factor that is required to find a desired item (function) in a table. For example, in the square root function SQRT(X), X is the argument. The value of X determines the square root value returned by this function.

array

1. An organized collection of data in which the argument is positioned before the function.

2. A group of items or elements in which the position of each item or element is significant. A multiplication table is a good example of an array.

ASCII

Acronym for American Standard Code for Information Interchange. ASCII is a standardized 8-bit code used by most computers for interfacing.

ASCII was developed by the American National Standards Institute (ANSI). It uses 7 binary bits for information and the 8th bit for parity purposes.

assembler

A computer program that produces a machine-language program which may then be directly executed by the computer.

assembly language

A symbolic language that is machine-oriented rather than problem-oriented. A program in an assembly language is converted by an assembler to a machine-language program. Symbols representing storage locations are converted to numerical storage locations; symbolic operation codes are converted to numeric operation codes.

asynchronous

1. Not having a regular time or clocked relationship. See *synchronous*.

2. A type of computer operation in which a new instruction is initiated when the former instruction is completed. Thus, there is no regular time schedule, or clock, with respect to instruction sequence. The current instruction must be complete before the next is begun, regardless of the length of time the current instruction takes.

asynchronous communication

A way of transmitting data serially from one device to another, in which each transmitted character is preceded by a start bit and followed by a stop bit. This is also called start/stop transmission.

back up

1. A second copy of data on a diskette or other medium, ensuring recovery from loss or destruction of the original media.

2. On-site or remote equipment available to complete an operation in the event of primary equipment failure.

BASIC

Acronym for Beginner's All-purpose Symbolic Instruction Code. BASIC is a computer programming language developed at Dartmouth College as an instructional tool in teaching fundamental programming concepts. This language has since gained wide acceptance as a time-sharing language and is considered one of the easiest programming languages to learn.

batch processing

A method of operating a computer so that a single program or set of related programs must be completed before the next type of program is begun.

baud

A unit of measurement of data processing speed. The speed in bauds is the number of signal elements per second. Since a signal element can represent more than one bit, baud is not synonymous with bits-per-second. Typical baud rates are 110, 300, 1200, 2400, 4800, and 9600.

binary

1. A characteristic or property involving a choice or condition in which there are two possibilities.

2. A numbering system which uses 2 as its base instead of 10 as in the decimal system. The binary system uses only two digits, 0 and 1, in its written form.

3. A device whose design uses only two possible states or levels to perform its functions. A computer executes programs in binary form.

binary digit

A quantity which is expressed in the binary digits of 0 and 1.

bit

A contraction of "binary digit". A bit can either be 0 or 1, and is the smallest unit of information recognizable by a computer.

block

An amount of storage space or data, of arbitrary length, usually contiguous, and often composed of several similar records, all of which are handled as a unit.

boolean logic

A field of mathematical analysis in which comparisons are made. A programmed instruction can cause a comparison of two fields of data, and modify one of those fields or another field as a result of comparison. This system was formulated by British mathematician George Boole (1815-1864). Some boolean operators are OR, AND, NOT, XOR, EQV, and IMP.

boot

A machine procedure that allows a system to begin operations at the desired level by means of its own initiation. The first few instructions are loaded into a computer from an input device. These instructions allow the rest of the system to be loaded. The word *boot* is abbreviated from the word *bootstrap*.

bps

Bits per second.

buffer

A temporary storage area from which data is transferred to or from various devices.

built-in clock

A real-time clock that lets your programs use the time of day and date. Built into MS-DOS, it lets you set the timing of a program. It can be used to keep a personal calendar, and it automatically measures elapsed time.

byte

An element of data which is composed of eight data bits plus a parity bit, and represents either one alphabetic or special character, two decimal digits, or eight binary bits. Byte is also used to refer to a sequence of eight binary digits handled as a unit. It is usually encoded in the *ASCII* format.

calculation

A series of numbers and mathematical signs that, when entered into a computer, is executed according to a series of instructions.

central processor (CPU)

The heart of the computer system, where data is manipulated and calculations are performed. The CPU contains a control unit to interpret and execute the program and an arithmetic-logic unit to perform computations and logical processes. It also routes information, controls input and output, and temporarily stores data.

chaining

The use of a pointer in a record to indicate the address of another record logically related to the first.

character

Any single letter of the alphabet, numeral, punctuation mark, or other symbol that a computer can read, write, and store. Character is synonymous with the term *byte*.

COBOL

Acronym for COmmon Business-Oriented Language, a computer language suitable for writing complicated business applications programs. It was developed by CODASYL, a committee representing the U. S. Department of Defense, certain computer manufacturers, and major users of data processing equipment. COBOL is designed to express data manipulations and processing problems in English narrative form, in a precise and standard manner.

code

1. To write instructions for a computer system
2. To classify data according to arbitrary tables
3. To use a machine language
4. To program

command

A pulse, signal, word, or series of letters that tells a computer to start, stop, or continue an operation in an instruction. Command is often used incorrectly as a synonym for *instruction*.

compatible

A description of data, programs or equipment that can be used between different kinds of computers or equipment.

compiler

A computer program that translates a program written in a problem-oriented language into a program of instructions similar to, or in, the language of the computer.

computer network

A geographically dispersed configuration of computer equipment connected by communication lines and capable of load sharing, distributive processing, and automatic communication between the computers within the network.

concatenate

To join together data sets, such as files, in a series to form one data set, such as one new file. The term concatenate literally means "to link together." A concatenated data set is a collection of logically connected data sets.

configuration

In hardware, a group of interrelated devices that constitute a system. In software, the total of the software modules and their interrelationships.

constant

A never-changing value or data item.

coprocessor

A microprocessor device connected to a central microprocessor that performs specialized computations (such as floating-point arithmetic) much more efficiently than the CPU alone.

cursor

A blinking line or box on a computer screen that indicates the next location for data entry.

data

A general term used to signify all the basic information elements that can be produced or processed by a computer. See *information*.

data element

The smallest named physical data unit.

data file

A collection of related data records organized in a specific manner. Data files contain computer records which contain information, as opposed to containing data handling information or a program.

debug

The process of checking the logic of a computer program to isolate and remove mistakes from the program or other software.

default

An action or value that the computer automatically assumes, unless a different instruction or value is given.

delimit

To establish parameters; to set a minimum and a maximum.

delimiter

A character that marks the beginning or end of a unit of data on a storage medium. Commas, semi-colons, periods, and spaces are used as delimiters to separate and organize items of data.

detail file

A data file composed of records having similar characteristics, but containing data which is relatively changeable by nature, such as employee weekly payroll data. Compare to *master file*.

device

A piece of hardware that can perform a specific function. A printer is an example of a device.

diagnostic programs

Special programs used to align equipment or isolate equipment malfunctions.

directory

A table that gives the name, location, size, and the creation or last revision date for each file on the storage media.

diskette

A flat, flexible platter coated with magnetic material, enclosed in a protective envelope, and used for storage of software and data.

Disk Operating System

A collection of procedures and techniques that enable the computer to operate using a disk drive system for data entry and storage. Disk Operating System is usually abbreviated to *DOS*.

DOS

The acronym for Disk Operating System. DOS rhymes with "boss."

double-density

A type of diskette that has twice the storage capacity of standard single-density diskettes.

double-precision

The use of two computer words to represent each number. This technique allows the use of twice as many digits as are normally available and is used when extra precision is needed in calculations.

double-sided

A term that refers to a diskette that can contain data on both surfaces of the diskette.

drive

A device that holds and manipulates magnetic media so that the CPU can read data from or write data to them.

end-of-file mark (EOF)

A symbol or machine equivalent that indicates that the last record of a file has been read.

erase

To remove or replace magnetized spots from a storage medium.

error message

An audible or visual indication of hardware or software malfunction or of an illegal data-entry attempt.

execute

To carry out an instruction or perform a routine.

exponent

A symbol written above a factor and on the right, telling how many times the factor is repeated. In the example of A^2, A is the factor and 2 is the exponent. A^2 means A times A (A $\times$ A).

extension

A one-to-three-character set that follows a filename. The extension further defines or clarifies the filename. It is separated from the filename by a period(.).

field

An area of a record that is allocated for a specific category of data.

file

A collection of related data or programs that is treated as a unit by the computer.

file protection

The devices or procedures that prevent unintentional erasure of data on a storage device, such as a diskette.

file structure

A conceptual representation of how data values, records, and files are related to each other. The structure usually implies how the data is stored and how the data must be processed.

filename

The unique name, usually assigned by a user, that identifies one file for all subsequent operations that use that file.

fixed disk

A hard disk enclosed in a permanently-sealed housing that protects it from environmental interference. Used for storage of data.

floating-point arithmetic

A method of calculation in which the computer or program automatically records, and accounts for, the location of the radix point. The programmer need not consider the radix location.

floating-point routine

A set of program instructions that permits a floating-point mathematics operation in a computer which lacks the feature of automatically accounting for the radix point.

format

A predetermined arrangement of data that structures the storage of information on an external storage device.

function

A computer action, as defined by a specific instruction. Some GW-BASIC functions are COS, EOF, INSTR, LEFT\$, and TAN.

function keys

Specific keys on the keyboard that, when pressed, instruct the computer to perform a particular operation. The function of the keys is determined by the applications program being used.

GIGO

An informal term that indicates sloppy data processing; an acronym for Garbage In Garbage Out. The term GIGO is normally used to make the point that if the input data is bad (garbage in) then the output data will also be bad (garbage out).

global search

Used in reference to a variable (character or command), a global search causes the computer to locate all occurrences of that variable.

graphics

A hardware/software capability to display objects in pictures, rather than words, usually on a graphic (CRT) display terminal with line-drawing capability and permitting interaction, such as the use of a light pen.

hard copy

A printed copy of computer output in a readable form, such as reports, checks, or plotted graphs.

hardware

The physical equipment that comprises a system.

hexadecimal

A number system with a base, or radix, of 16. The symbols used in this system are the decimal digits 0 through 9 and six additional digits which are generally represented as A, B, C, D, E, and F.

hidden files

Files that cannot be seen during normal directory searches.

hierarchical directories

See *tree-structured directories.*

housekeeping functions

Routine operations that must be performed before the actual processing begins or after it is complete.

information

Facts and knowledge derived from data. The computer operates on and generates data. The meaning derived from the data is information; that is, information results from data. The two words are not synonymous, although they are often used interchangeably.

interpreter

A program that reads, translates and executes a user's program, such as one written in the BASIC language, one line at a time. A compiler, on the other hand, reads and translates the entire user's program before executing it.

input

1. The process or device concerning the entry of data into a computer.

2. Actual data being entered into a computer.

input/output

A general term for devices that communicate with a computer. Input/output is usually abbreviated as I/O.

instruction

A program step that tells the computer what to do next. Instruction is often used incorrectly as a synonym for command.

integer

A complete entity, having no fractional part. The whole or natural number. For example, 65 is an integer; 65.1 is not.

integrated circuit

A complete electronic circuit contained in a small semiconductor component.

interface

An information interchange path that allows parts of a computer, computers, and external equipment (such as printers, monitors, or modems), or two or more computers to communicate or interact.

I/O

The acronym for input/output.

job

A collection of tasks viewed by the computer as a unit.

K

The symbol signifying the quantity 2^{10}, which is equal to 1024. K is sometimes confused with the symbol k (kilo), which is equal to 1000.

logarithm

A logarithm of a given number is the value of the exponent indicating the power required to raise a specified constant, known as the base, to produce that given number. That is, if B is the base, N is the given number and L is the logarithm, then BL = N. Since 10^3 = 1000, the logarithm to the base 10 of 1000 is 3.

loop

A series of computer instructions that are executed repeatedly until a desired result is obtained or a predetermined condition is met. The ability to loop and reuse instructions eliminates countless repetitious instructions and is one of the most important attributes of stored programs.

M

The symbol signifying the quantity 1,000,000 (10^6). When used to denote storage, it more precisely refers to 1,048,576 (2^{20}).

mantissa

The fractional or decimal part of a logarithm of a number. For example, the logarithm of 163 is 2.212. The mantissa is 0.212, and the characteristic is 2.0.

In floating-point numbers, the mantissa is the number part. For example, the number 24 can be written as 24,2 where 24 is the mantissa and 2 is the exponent. The floating-point number is read as $.24 \times 10^2$, or 2^4.

master file

A data file composed of records having similar characteristics that rarely change. A good example of a master file would be an employee name and address file that also contains social security numbers and hiring dates.

media

The plural of medium.

medium

The physical material on which data is recorded and stored. Magnetic tape, punched cards, and diskettes are examples of media.

memory

The high-speed work area in the computer where data can be held, copied, and retrieved.

menu

A list of choices from which an operator can select a task or operation to be performed by the computer.

microprocessor

A semiconductor *central processing unit* (CPU) in a computer.

modem

Acronym for modulator demodulator. A modem converts data from a computer to analog signals that can be transmitted through telephone lines, or converts the signals from telephone lines into a form the computer can use.

MS-DOS

Acronym for Microsoft Disk Operating System.

nested programs or subroutines

A program or subroutine that is incorporated into a larger routine to permit ready execution or access of each level of the routine. For example, nesting loops involves incorporating one loop of instructions into another loop.

null

Empty or having no members. This is in contrast to a blank or zero, which indicates the presence of no information. For example, in the number 540, zero contains needed information.

numeric

A reference to numerals as opposed to letters or other symbols.

octal number system

A representation of values or quantities with octal numbers. The octal number system uses eight digits: 0, 1, 2, 3, 4, 5, 6, and 7, with each position in an octal numeral representing a power of 8. The octal system is used in computing as a simple means of expressing binary quantities.

operand

A quantity or data item involved in an operation. An operand is usually designated by the address portion of an instruction, but it may also be a result, a parameter, or an indication of the name or location of the next instruction to be executed.

operating system

An organized group of computer *instructions* that manage the overall operation of the computer.

operator

A symbol indicating an operation and itself the subject of the operation. It indicates the process that is being performed. For example, + is addition, − is subtraction, × is multiplication, and / is division.

option

An add-on device that expands a system's capabilities.

output

Computer results, or data that has been processed.

parallel output

The method by which all bits of a binary word are transmitted simultaneously.

parameter

A *variable* that is given a value for a specific program or run. A definable characteristic of an item, device, or system.

parity

An extra-bit of code that is used to detect data errors in memory by making the sum of the active bit in a data word either an odd or an even number.

partition

An area on a *fixed disk* set aside for a specific purpose, such as a location for an operating system.

peripheral

An external input/output, or storage device.

pixel

The acronym for picture element. A pixel is a single dot on a monitor that can be addressed by a single bit.

port

The entry channel to and from the central computer for connection of a communications line or other *peripheral* device.

power

The functional area of a system that transforms an external power source into internal DC supply voltage.

program

A series of instructions or statements in a form acceptable to a computer, designed to cause the computer to execute a series of operations. Computer programs include software such as operating systems, assemblers, compilers, interpreters, data management systems, utility programs, sort-merge programs, and maintenance/diagnostic programs, as well as application programs such as payroll, inventory control, and engineering analysis programs.

prompt

A character or series of characters that appear on the screen to request input from the user.

RAM

Acronym for *random-access memory.*

radian

The natural unit of measure of the angle between two intersecting half-lines on the angles from one half-line to another intersecting half-line. It is the angle subtended by an arc of a circle equal in length to the radius of the circle. As the circumference of a circle is equal to 2π times its radius, the number of radians in an angle of 360° or in a complete turn is 2π.

radix

A number that is arbitrarily made the fundamental number of a system of numbers; a base. Thus, 10 is the radix, or base, of the common system of logarithms, and also of the decimal system of enumeration.

random-access memory

The system's high-speed work area that provides access to memory storage locations by using a system of vertical and horizontal coordinates. The computer can write information into or read information from the random-access memory. Random-access memory is often called *RAM*.

raster unit

On a graphic display screen, a raster unit is the horizontal or vertical distance between two adjacent addressable points on the screen.

read-only memory

A type of memory that contains permanent data or instructions. The computer can read from but not write to the read-only memory. Read-only memory is often called *ROM*.

real number

An ordinary number, either rational or irrational; a number in which there is no imaginary part, a number generated from the single unit, 1; any point in a continuum of natural numbers filled in with all rationals and all irrationals and extended indefinitely, both positive and negative.

real time

1. The actual time required to solve a problem.

2. The process of solving a problem during the actual time that a related physical process takes place so that results can be used to guide the physical process.

remote

A term used to refer to devices that are located at sites away from the central computer.

reverse video

A display of characters on a background, opposite of the usual display.

ROM

Acronym for *read-only memory*.

RS-232

A standard communications interface between a *modem* and terminal devices that complies with EIA Standard RS-232.

serial output

Sending only one bit at a time to and from interconnected devices.

single-density

The standard recording density of a diskette. Single-density diskettes can store approximately 3400 bits per inch (bpi).

single-precision value

The number of words or storage positions used to denote a number in a computer. Single-precision arithmetic is the use of one word per number, double-precision arithmetic is the use of two words per number, and so on. For variable word-length computers, precision is the number of digits used to denote a number. The higher the precision, the greater the number of decimal places that can be carried.

single-sided

A term used to describe a diskette that contains data on one side only.

software

A string of instructions that, when executed, direct the computer to perform certain functions.

stack architecture

An architecture wherein any portion of the external memory can be used as a last-in, first-out stack to store/retrieve the contents of the accumulator, the flags, or any of the data registers. Many units contain a 16-bit stack pointer to control the addressing of this external stack. One of the major advantages of the stack is that multiple-level interrupts can be handled easily, since complete system status can be saved when an interrupt occurs and then be restored after the interrupt. Another major advantage is that almost unlimited subroutine nesting is possible.

statement

A high-level language instruction to the computer to perform some sequence of operations.

synchronous

A type of computer operation in which the execution of each instruction or each event is controlled by a clock signal: evenly spaced pulses that enable the logic gates for the execution of each logic step. A synchronous operation can cause time delays by causing waiting for clock signals although all other signals at a particular logic gate were available. See *asynchronous*.

switch

An instruction, added to a command, that designates a course of action, other than default, for the command process to follow.

syntax

Rules of statement structure in a programming language.

system

A collection of hardware, software, and firmware that is interconnected to operate as a unit.

task

A machine run; a program in execution.

toggle

Alternation of function between two stable states.

track

A specific area on a moving-storage medium, such as a diskette, disk, or tape cartridge, that can be accessed by the drive heads.

tree-structured directory

A file-organization structure, consisting of directories and subdirectories that, when diagrammed, resembles a tree.

truncation

To end a computation according to a specified rule; for example, to drop numbers at the end of a line instead of rounding them off, or to drop characters at the end of a line when a file is copied.

upgrade

To expand a system by installing options or using revised software.

utility function

Computer programs, dedicated to one particular task, that are helpful in using the computer. For example, FDISK, for setting up partitions on the fixed disk.

variable

A quantity that can assume any of a set of values as a result of processing data.

volume label

The name for the contents of a diskette or a partition on a fixed disk.

word

The set of bits comprising the largest unit that the computer can handle in a single operation.

write-protect notch

A cut-out opening in the sealed envelope of a diskette that, when covered, prevents writing or adding text to the diskette, but allows information to be read from the diskette.

INDEX

Index

Index

A Word About Microsoft® QuickBASIC

Learn BASIC the QuickBASIC way and discover the advantages of modern-structured programming techniques. The Microsoft QuickBASIC Interpreter combines powerful, state-of-the-art features—such as automatic error checking and correction—with innovations that make BASIC programming easy to learn, including drop-down menus, on-line help, and easy-editing capabilities. It's a powerful subset of Microsoft GW-BASIC.

**350 pages,
softcover with
three 5.25-inch disks
7 ³/₈ x 9 ¹/₄ $39.95
Order Code LEBANO**

LEARN BASIC NOW
Mike Halvorson and David Rygmyr
Foreword by Bill Gates

LEARN BASIC NOW is an exciting new approach to learning BASIC programming quickly and easily. LEARN BASIC NOW comes complete with the speedy Microsoft QuickBASIC Interpreter, top-notch electronic help resources, and outstanding on-line and book tutorials. With little or no programming experience, you can learn how to program in BASIC on an IBM PC or compatible, using LEARN BASIC NOW. This completely integrated system is guaranteed to make BASIC programming easy as it is useful to know. Everything you need to learn structured programming with BASIC is on the three 5.25-inch disks and in the companion book. Included in this package are:

■ The Microsoft QuickBASIC Interpreter. This fast, full-featured interpreter—a $39.95 value—makes learing to program in BASIC easy and enjoyable.

■ The Microsoft QBI Express. This on-line tutorial introduces you to the Microsoft QuickBASIC Interpreter.

■ The Microsoft QBI Advisor. Simply press a key or click your mouse to reach this electronic help system instantly! Hypertext-based cross-referencing lets you work through related topics in a flash.

■ Sample Programs. Dozens of programs—on disk and in the book—provide a superb introduction to good programming techniques. They're both useful *and* fun!

■ Companion Book. This solid, hands-on tutorial offers an introduction to BASIC programming concepts and a detailed look at writing BASIC programs with the Microsoft QuickBASIC Interpreter. Review questions and answers in each chapter test your progress.

LEARN BASIC NOW—a great way to learn a great language!

PROGRAMMERS AT WORK
Interviews with 19 Programmers Who Shaped the Computer Industry
Susan Lammers

PROGRAMMERS AT WORK is a collection of captivating interviews that probe the minds of 19 of the software industry's most notable programmers. The interviews highlight the forces, the events, and the personalities of today's software movers and shakers. How do these programmers approach program design? Is programming a talent or a learned skill? An art or a science? And how do these programmers envision the future of computing? Although each interview reveals an individual success story, the collection taken as a whole provides a colorful portrait of the microcomputer industry. Included are interviews with Andy Hertzfeld (Macintosh Operating System), John Warnock (PostScript), C. Wayne Ratliff (dBASE), Jonathan Sachs (Lotus 1-2-3), and Bill Gates (BASIC). A lively appendix provides some actual code and worksheets from these software wizards.

400 pages, softcover   7 ³/₈ x 9 ¹/₄ $9.95   Order Code PRWOTE

Available wherever books and software are sold. Or order directly from Microsoft Press.

From the DOS Experts...